Marxism

Marxism
A Post–Cold War Primer

Markar Melkonian

⛬ WestviewPress
A Division of HarperCollins*Publishers*

All rights reserved. Printed in the United States of America. No part of this publication may be reproduced or transmitted in any form or by any means, electronic or mechanical, including photocopy, recording, or any information storage and retrieval system, without permission in writing from the publisher.

Copyright © 1994, 1996 by Markar Melkonian

Published in 1996 in the United States of America by Westview Press, 5500 Central Avenue, Boulder, Colorado 80301-2877, and in the United Kingdom by Westview Press, 12 Hid's Copse Road, Cumnor Hill, Oxford OX2 9JJ

Library of Congress Cataloging-in-Publication Data
Melkonian, Markar.
  Marxism: a post–Cold War primer / Markar Melkonian.
    p. cm.
  Includes bibliographical references and index.
  ISBN 0-8133-2885-3.—ISBN 0-8133-2886-1 (pbk.)
  1. Communism. 2. Post-communism. I. Title.
HX73.M45 1996
335.43—dc20
                                                                                      96-15151
                                                                                                            CIP

The paper used in this publication meets the requirements of the American National Standard for Permanence of Paper for Printed Library Materials Z39.48-1984.

10   9   8   7   6   5   4   3   2   1

*To Sureya
and the children of the Intifada*

Contents

Preface ix

Introduction: The Weapon of Theory 1

1 What Makes Marxist Theory Scientific? 7

Marxist Theory Is Materialist, 8
Marxism Differs from Other Forms of Materialism, 17
Objections to the View that Marxism Is Scientific, 19
Summary, 21
Reading List, 22
Founders of Historical Materialism:
 Karl Marx and Friedrich Engels, 23
Notes, 24

2 What Is a Society? 27

Society as a Structure Made Up of Practices, 28
Modes of Production, 33
Class, 40
Summary, 46
Reading List, 47
Founders of Historical Materialism:
 Vladimir Ilyich Lenin, 48
Notes, 50

3 The Capitalist Mode of Production 51

Commodity Production, 51
Capitalist Exploitation, 55
Capital, 61
Summary, 65
Reading List, 66

Founders of Historical Materialism: Rosa Luxemburg, 67
Notes, 69

4 The Capitalist State and Ideology   71

States and Ruling Classes, 71
Ideology, 77
Is the Concept of a Ruling Class Obsolete? 82
Summary, 86
Reading List, 87
Founders of Historical Materialism: Antonio Gramsci, 88
Notes, 89

5 Imperialism   91

The Monopoly Stage of Capitalism, 91
The International Capitalist System, 96
Imperialism Versus Peace and the Environment, 103
Summary, 107
A Note on Further Readings, 108
Marxists of Africa: Walter Rodney, 109
Notes, 110

6 What Do Marxists Fight For?   113

Socialism, 114
Learning from Defeats, 120
Communism, 125
Summary, 128
Reading List, 129
Three Fighting Marxists: Elizabeth Gurley Flynn,
   Ho Chi Minh, and Che Guevara, 129
Notes, 131

Glossary   133
About the Book and Author   141
Index   143

Preface

I can remember "correctly" answering a test question in a junior high school textbook: How do we know Karl Marx was wrong? Presumably, any eighth grader who had read the short section about communism in the textbook was prepared to fire back the correct answer: "Because Marx said there was going to be a revolution in England, and this didn't happen." Full stop, move on to the next "ism." A couple of years later, when a wave of antiunion violence swept over the fields and farm labor camps of California's San Joaquin Valley where I was born and raised, I began to read Marx for myself and came to my own conclusions.

Marxism has been declared dead a hundred times and has supposedly been refuted by one hundred different arguments. There have been "post-Marxists" at least since the 1920s, when an author named Henri DeMan wrote a now long-forgotten book entitled *Beyond Marx.* And I recall that the editor of the edition of the *Communist Manifesto* I read as a youth claimed that Marx wrote his four-volume work, *Capital,* just so that his followers could point to some big heavy books on a shelf as the source of their religious beliefs. I have even heard a man who believes in angels describe Marxism as an "absurd ideology"!

This description raises a number of questions: If Marxism is indeed an absurd ideology, then why do non-Marxist economists, sociologists, and historians worry about it so much? And if this doctrine is bankrupt, then why does it continue to attract some of the brightest champions of the exploited majority of the human population of our planet? And a further question will crop up during the course of this book: If Marxism is an obsolete, absurd ideology, then why do the opponents of Marxism time and again fight against Marxists by censoring them and misrepresenting their views? After all, assuming one has faith in the ability of well-informed people to make reasonable choices, one would think that the best way to combat an absurd ideology would be to present that ideology accurately, in all its absurdity.

Today, as I write these lines, the opponents of Marxism have never had it so good. The self-described socialist regimes of eastern Europe have toppled like dead trees, and their old, self-serving party bosses have either fallen in disgrace or been reborn as nationalists and budding capitalists. Behind us is what professors, politicians, and publicists in the West gleefully proclaim to have been the collapse of communism.

In Chapter 6 it will become clear that this title is inaccurate: What collapsed in the late 1980s was not at all what Marx and Lenin would have called communism. It is not surprising, however, that pro-capitalist intellectuals, from the far right to today's fashionable "post-Marxists," do not bother to challenge the accuracy of the term "collapse of communism." And it is not surprising that they have not bothered to question the socialist credentials of the regimes and parties that fell in eastern Europe, the former Soviet Union, and elsewhere. By taking the word of the dictators of Romania and Albania that theirs were genuinely socialist countries, political leaders in capitalist countries and their millionaire media have been able to put Marxists in their own countries on the defensive.

The professors, politicians, and publicists have much to celebrate now that attempts to build socialism in the twentieth century have been defeated. And yet, judging by their continuing efforts to silence Marxists in labor unions, universities, and elsewhere, those who celebrate what they like to call the collapse of communism evidently do not trust their own declarations that Marxism has discredited itself everywhere and for all time.

The problem some of the more farsighted capitalists might suspect is that capitalism itself has a way of putting socialism back on the agenda. The new capitalist rulers of eastern Europe have brought with them hunger, unemployment, "ethnic cleansing," greater oppression of women, greedy commercialism, political deception, deeper and deeper poverty for the majority, and a growing gap between rich and poor. Sooner or later, a new generation of workers in eastern Europe and elsewhere will face up to the reality of class conflict. And when this happens, we can expect some of them to reexamine Marxism fairly and come to their own conclusions.

In the meantime, I offer this primer to those who are not satisfied with the self-serving arguments of the small number of people who are making a killing off of what they are pleased to call the collapse of communism.

*   *   *

The reading lists included at the ends of the chapters in this book make up a program of further study. I have tried to limit selections to books currently in print or to books that can be found in any of the larger public or university libraries in the United States. Many of these books, especially the Marxist-Leninist classics, have been brought out by more than one publisher, in more than one edition, and sometimes under different titles. An item preceded by an asterisk(*) should be considered required reading.

I have three tips about how to read this material: First of all, reread it. Books like the first volume of *Capital* require more than one reading. Second, if at all possible, regularly discuss what you read with others. A good way to do this is to form small study groups. Even the most informal study group has an advantage over studying alone. Finally, study-group leaders (as well as authors of primers on Marxism!) should keep in mind that the job of educating oneself is never over—there is always a need for further study. As Marx noted in the third of his *Theses on Feuerbach,* the educator must himself be educated.[1]

During the course of writing this primer, I have benefited greatly from discussions with friends, students, and comrades. John Brentlinger and Geoff Goshgarian graciously read the rough draft and criticized it in detail, and, over the course of long hours of discussion, Kanchana Mahadevan helped me to clarify many of my positions. It's safe to say that none of these individuals would lay claim to each and every view contained in this little book. As I point out in the Introduction, there is a wide range of opinion among Marxists. It is even safer to say, however, that this primer is in much better shape, thanks to their generous assistance.

Markar Melkonian

Notes

1. The *Theses on Feuerbach* are included in David McLellan, ed., *Karl Marx: Selected Writings* (Oxford: Oxford University Press, 1977), pp. 156–158.

Marxism

Introduction: The Weapon of Theory

Marx, in his scientific creation, has outstripped us as a party of practical fighters. It is not true that Marx no longer suffices for our needs. On the contrary, our needs are not yet adequate for using Marx's ideas.
—Rosa Luxemburg, 1903

Often when they pretend to discuss Marxism, professors and writers in the West set up their own caricature of Marxist theory and then ceremoniously proceed to knock it down. They then pronounce themselves the victors and receive heartfelt congratulations from their colleagues.

Thus, for example, some pro-capitalist writers recast Marxism in the image of an easily defeated view that goes by the big name of *technological determinism*. According to this caricature, history is reduced to a long process of technical innovation for the sake of producing more goods faster. This technical innovation more or less automatically triggers social "progress." To put a crude view crudely, the smelting of metals gave rise to slavery, the power loom put an end to feudalism, and the steam engine spawned industrial capitalism. Or so the caricature goes.

There is little we can do about this sort of misrepresentation of Marxist theory except to call attention to it when the opportunity arises. This primer presents a very different view of Marxism, one that is much closer to the views of the founders of the new science of history and society that has come to be known as historical materialism. As will become clear when we turn to the issue of ideology in Chapter 4, if Marxism were usually presented in a fair manner in capitalist societies, this fact itself would indicate that there is something wrong with the Marxist theory of ideology.

Unfortunately, some self-proclaimed Marxists have abetted those who draw crude caricatures of Marxism. The worst of these so-called Marxists were the authors of the uninspired official Soviet textbooks and pamphlets on "Scientific Communism." One genuinely good result of the collapse of the Soviet Union is that young people are no longer required to read Stalin's *History of the Communist Party of the Soviet Union—Short Course*[1] and similar more recent textbooks. In the past, many thoughtful students have rejected the "orthodox" views contained in this literature. Unfortunately, however, most of these students have accepted the false claim that these were accurate popular presentations of historical materialism.

Orthodox is a word we use to describe churches and religious dogmas, not scientific theories. We are not surprised to hear about orthodox Suni Muslims or the Russian Orthodox Church, but people don't usually talk about orthodox biologists or geologists. In Chapter 1, we will see that Marxist theory is more like biology or geology than a religious faith, a fact that people who call themselves orthodox Marxists do not seem to recognize.

There have been different versions of orthodox Marxism, just as there are different versions of orthodox Hinduism. But one of the common claims of the orthodox Marxists is that the economy determines the way people think and the form of their government more or less in the way a three-dimensional figure determines the shape of its shadow. As we have seen, this is also the view of the technological determinists.

Moreover, as it turns out, it is also an old familiar claim of what have accurately been called revisionist Marxists. Revisionists of various stripes believe that even the most general concepts and claims of historical materialism need to be updated, usually by trying to shove Marxism into the mold of the latest philosophical fashion in the West. Marxism for the revisionists is like wet plaster.

Defenders of orthodoxy, by contrast, see Marxism as a static doctrine, a sitting duck that needs to be shielded from potshots rather than developed and taken seriously as an emerging science of history and society.

Referring to Marxists, Lenin once wrote: "We do not regard Marx's theory as something completed and inviolable; on the contrary, we are convinced that it has only laid the foundation stone of the science which socialists *must* develop in all directions if they wish to keep pace with life."[2] Lenin's lifework reflected this belief—

Introduction: The Weapon of Theory

although the same cannot be said of many of those who later claimed his heritage. Marxist theory is neither wet plaster nor a sitting duck. It is more like a shark that must keep moving to stay alive. To cast Marxism as a finished and closed set of beliefs is to repeat the disastrous trends of the past, penning up Marxist theory in stagnant water and in that way suffocating and killing it.

This leads to another point, a point that the editors of Soviet textbooks such as the *Short Course* usually ignored: There has been and continues to be a wide range of opinions and debate within the larger Marxist tradition. This primer is written for beginners who probably are not aware of how wide the range is. Nevertheless, students who go on to study historical materialism more deeply should be forewarned of the variety and even conflict among many Marxist and Marxist-Leninist thinkers.

I have tried to inform myself about some of the more important debates raging within Marxism, to weigh them fairly, and to present to students the most accurate and coherent interpretation I know. Nevertheless, every reader of this primer should bear in mind that the interpretation I present is one of many and that other interpretations deserve to be considered, too.

To repeat, then, orthodox Marxists, like the authors of the old Soviet textbooks as well as revisionists like Henri DeMan, who would like us to believe that they have passed beyond Marxism, see Marxism as a closed and completed doctrine, to be either defended or attacked as such, which, as we will see is a very inaccurate picture. Marx's biographer Franz Mehring noted that even as a young man in his early twenties, before Marx was a "Marxist," he set himself against the attempt to settle all problems for all time. And many years later, frustrated by the claims of his French followers that Marxism provides cut-and-dry answers to all questions, past, present, and future, Marx complained, "All I know is that I am not a Marxist!"[3]

This little book was written in the belief that those of us who call ourselves Marxists should try as best we can to contribute to the development of Marxist theory without distorting its most general claims and concepts. This belief applies even—or especially—to a primer such as this. The proposed task, however, is more easily described than accomplished. A descriptive rundown of the "high points" of historical materialism cannot help but be a misrepresentation, at least to some extent, for two reasons.

First of all, the concepts of historical materialism depend for their meaning on their interrelation. As we will see, for example, what is important is the relationship between labor-power and labor, abstract labor and concrete labor, relations of production and forces of production, economic relations and political institutions.

Second, like the science of physics four centuries ago or evolutionary biology earlier in this century, historical materialism is currently feeling the heat of class struggle. In his play *The Life of Galileo*, Bertolt Brecht pointed out that capitalist merchants in seventeenth-century Italy supported Galileo because, among other reasons, they wanted to weaken the power of the Church and the feudal rulers who were interfering with the new capitalists' business. Galileo's physics, then, became a theoretical weapon in the hands of the rising merchant-capitalist class. The Church and the feudal rulers recognized this, and they used their influence and power to misrepresent Galileo's physical theory and to silence him.

At this point, however, a warning is in order: To think of Galileo's physics—or any other scientific theory—as a weapon in the hands of one class or another can easily lead to misunderstandings. For one thing, no scientific theory is a finished object that, once forged, need only be picked up and wielded against one's enemies. If physics and historical materialism are weapons, then they are always-unfinished weapons—weapons constantly being reforged in the midst of battle and constantly in danger of being bent, dropped, or dismantled.

Furthermore, the fate of these theories is tied to the fate of the combatants. In the case of Galileo, as we know, the Church was temporarily victorious, forcing him to recant his theories. As a result, Galileo's work did not initially reach as wide a public as it might have. This could not help but have retarded research into the new physics, at least in southern Europe. Similarly, censorship and repression in the West as well as in the defunct orthodox Marxist regimes in the East have retarded the development of Marxist theory in the twentieth century.

There is another reason some Marxists bristle at the suggestion that Marxism is a weapon: They point out that a weapon, like any other tool, has a use only in relation to a preset task. Tools help to "get the job done." Historical materialism, by contrast, helps us to determine just what that "job" is that needs to be done.

For example, by helping us to understand the role that capitalism plays in propping up racism in many societies, Marxism helps us to

Introduction: The Weapon of Theory

understand that the most enduring and far-reaching victories over racism are tied to the fight against capitalist exploitation. Or, to take an example to which we will return in Chapter 5, by drawing connections between advanced capitalism and environmental pollution, Marxism can help environmentalists identify their goals more realistically. Marxism is also crucial for defining goals of labor movements, national liberation struggles, and other social movements aiming at revolutionary change.

To view historical materialism exclusively as a weapon or a tool is to view it one-sidedly. And to view historical materialism one-sidedly is to risk taking political goals for granted and seeing Marxism as little more than a means to ends that have been preset, perhaps by party bureaucrats in smoke-filled rooms.

Some Marxists believe that this danger is so great that it is a mistake to think of Marxism as a weapon at all. They may be right; nevertheless, I for one remain convinced that in an introductory text such as this it is particularly helpful in our present era of "pragmatism" to emphasize the connection between Marxism and political struggles—as long as we stress that historical materialism is also an emerging science. In an attempt to address the last concern and to be less one-sided, I chose to discuss the topic of Marxism as a science in Chapter 1 (even though I realize that a more satisfactory discussion of this topic would set out first to dispel the exaggerated aura of certainty surrounding many students' ideas about science).

* * *

The purpose of this primer is to provide beginning students with a framework for future systematic study of Marxist theory. If I am successful, the student who has read through this little book should have acquired a rough-and-ready picture of Marxist theory in its broadest outline. I will have done more harm than good, however, if students convince themselves that after reading these few pages they know all they need to know about Marxist theory.[4] At the end of each chapter I have suggested further readings to help fill in the rough outline I present.

Students should keep in mind, however, that reading even a hundred books will not be enough if they do not reflect on what is being read in light of the circumstances of their own lives. As they study Marxist theory further, students should ask themselves "personal" questions such as: Are either of my parents exploited? Am I? Can I make sense of Marxism even though I have a capitalist class background? Have Marxists pointed to problems that my schoolteachers, the news media, or the entertainment industry seem always to have ignored? If so, what are they?

Once we come to understand our societies and history better, it will become clear that things have not always been the way they happen to be at present. Just as social upheaval has taken place over and over again in the past, it will also take place in the future. Furthermore, those of us who are workers or who take a stand with exploited and oppressed people might very well come to the conclusion that, in Marx's famous words, "the point is to change it."[5]

Armed with the weapon of Marxist theory, Marxists can "change it." But first we need to familiarize ourselves with our weapons.

Notes

1. First published in Moscow in 1939.

2. V.I. Lenin, *Collected Works* Vol. 4 (Moscow: Progress Publishers, 1972), pp. 211–212.

3. Dona Torr, trans., *Karl Marx and Friedrich Engels: Selected Correspondence* (New York: International Publishers, 1942), p. 472.

4. In fact, I have tried to keep this primer as thin as possible in order to deprive readers of a feeling of accomplishment after having read it.

5. The eleventh and last of Marx's *Theses on Feuerbach* states: "The philosophers have only interpreted the world in various ways; the point is to change it." *Theses on Feuerbach*, in David McLellan, ed., *Karl Marx: Selected Writings* (Oxford: Oxford University Press, 1977), p. 158.

1

What Makes Marxist Theory Scientific?

It is not the conciousness of men that determines their being, but, on the contrary, their social being that determines their consciousness.

—*Karl Marx*

Marxists claim that Karl Marx built the framework for a scientific understanding of social change. But if Marxist theory is scientific, what makes it so?

It might seem strange to try to answer this question before we have a firmer idea of what Marxist theory is in the first place. It is helpful, however, to take a look at the "big picture," before turning to Marxist theory in greater detail in later chapters. In the course of considering what makes Marxist theory scientific, we'll take a brief look at the relationship between historical materialism and other sciences, such as physics and biology. Because this chapter is concerned with issues of a very general nature, issues having to do with relationships between various scientific fields, it will be more "philosophical" than the chapters that follow.

Before going further, however, we should be at least a little clearer about what we mean by *Marxist theory*. Some people have pictured Marxist theory as falling into two or more separate areas of study, including an economic theory and a theory of human history. According to this account, Marx's economic theory, which he worked out in his major work, *Capital*, is concerned with economic laws, whereas his writings on politics and history are concerned with the laws of class struggle.

This is not the best way to look at things. During the course of this book, it will be argued that Marxists should not study economic production separately from history, society, and politics. Marx and Engels's historical writings, including the *Eighteenth Brumaire of Louis Bonaparte* and the writings on the civil wars in France, are closely connected to their economic theories, and the two bodies of writing are part of their larger materialist conception of history.

It is true that Marx spent more time on his economic theory and worked it out in greater detail than he did any other part of his materialist conception of history. Nevertheless, later Marxists focused on other aspects of the larger theory, such as the connection between political institutions and the economy, studies of culture and dominant ways of thinking, discussions about the best methods for studying history and societies, and so on. Each of these fields of study is more or less developed—or undeveloped. Each is evolving over time and at different rates. Nevertheless, at least in the account of Marxism presented in this primer, each of these areas of study makes up part of Marx's materialist conception of history. For these reasons, we should view Marxist theory first and foremost as historical materialism, the materialist conception of history.

Marxist Theory Is Materialist

This book is a sketch in broad outline of Marx's materialist conception of history. Before proceeding, however, we should consider what Marxists mean when they say that Marx's theory is materialist. In this chapter, it should become clear that all genuinely scientific fields are consistent with materialism, even if it is not true that all scientists personally believe themselves to be materialists.

But what is materialism? Materialism is a trend in philosophy, or a general approach to the study of things. There have been many different schools of materialist philosophy in the East and the West. Despite their differences, however, all materialists subscribe to three very general claims or theses: (1) There are things other than thoughts and thinkers, (2) thoughts of objects or events are different from the actual objects or events about which something is thought, and (3) being determines consciousness—that is, objects and events in some sense have primacy over knowledge about them.

First, let us consider the claim that there are things other than thoughts and thinkers. According to this thesis, things exist and events take place outside people's heads. This view is sometimes called *philosophical realism*. All materialists are philosophical realists.

Let me illustrate what philosophical realism involves and what it doesn't involve by considering the relationship between humans and nature. In the process, I also hope to dispel one common misunderstanding about Marxism.

In general and with some exceptions, centuries of experience, innovation, and skill have enabled human groups to produce more food, shelter, and clothing in less time. Land has been cultivated, fields irrigated, forests cleared, dams built, and so on. In the past, many people, including some Marxists, have concluded from this fact that human history is a history of conquering, mastering, or humanizing nature. Underlying this claim is the deep-rooted belief, common to more than one religion, that God the Great Thinker created the world by thinking. So the world in a sense is God's thought. God also created humans. Unlike God's other creations, however, humans, created in God's image, are able to think. Because humans are able to think—because we are conscious—we are separate from nature, over which God has given us dominion. According to a more modern variation of this myth, nature is a foreign enemy against which humans must battle for supremacy in order to survive.

To repeat, these are not Marxist beliefs; rather, they are deeply rooted religious beliefs that some Marxists have uncritically adopted. Few people would deny that humans have always had to work to survive. It is an entirely different thing, however, to claim that all human labor up to the present time has amounted to a battle for supremacy over an external enemy, nature.

Some Marxists disagree. They point to the fact that, in section one of the *Communist Manifesto*, for example, the authors wrote about the "subjection of Nature's forces to man."[1] This and other quotations underscore the fact that as young men, Marx and Engels wrote in the style of the idealist philosophers of their day. Nevertheless, in their mature writings, Marx and Engels drew no neat line separating humans from the rest of nature. In the preface to *Capital*, for example, Marx declared that he viewed the evolution of the economic formation of society as a "process of natural history."[2] Indeed, in his book *Anti-Duhring*, Engels even stressed that "like any other species of animal on Earth, humans are still evolving and will eventually disappear."[3]

Some Marxists, influenced by the European Enlightenment, have looked upon nonhuman nature as just a source of raw materials to be transformed by human intelligence and labor. But surely nonhuman nature is more than just an object of human nature, the way the whole world is supposed to be an object of God's thought. Without natural resources to transform into raw materials through labor, humans could not produce what they need to survive. Marx emphasized this point in his *Critique of the Gotha Program* when he criticized the slogan that labor is the sole source of all wealth and insisted instead that nature is as necessary a condition for economic production as is labor.

To bring this point home, let's consider just a few well-established scientific beliefs:

- We inhabit part of the surface of a smaller-than-average planet in a solar system orbiting one medium-sized star on the edge of one galaxy among billions of other galaxies, each composed of billions of other stars. Most astronomers today believe that a vast explosion they call the big bang took place perhaps 15 billion years ago. The big bang, they believe, brought into existence the matter, space, and time that make up the universe. Since then, according to this account, the universe has been expanding and cooling.
- There is evidence that the planets of our solar system, including the earth, started to form some 4.5 billion years ago. And, as earthquakes and volcanoes remind us, our planet continues to change. Astronomers expect the sun to expand into a giant red star 5 billion years from now. When it does, it will consume the planets Mercury and Venus and burn up all life on our planet.
- The human species, *Homo sapiens,* is one of tens of millions of interdependent species of plants and animals on Earth. Today, paleontologists (scientists who study fossils) pretty much agree that the species *Homo sapiens* has existed in more or less the present form for at least 100,000 years, and some believe *Homo sapiens* might have existed as far back as 400,000 years ago. But even if we accept the older date, this would mean that our species has existed for less than one one-hundredth of one percent (.01%) of the time Earth has existed.

It is always possible, of course, that astronomers, biologists, and paleontologists may in the future arrive at a different view of things. In any case, however, there is an enormous amount of evidence that stars, the earth, and innumerable other things existed for a long time before humans made their appearance on the scene and will continue to exist long after we are gone. In view of all of this, it seems silly—and perhaps a bit sad—to hear some people continue to claim that humans are conquering nature or "humanizing the world."

Of course, if, as the German philosopher Johann Fichte said, the world is my idea, then I could make the case that domination of nature is just domination of my own ideas. After all, once I accept the view that galaxies and stars are just my idea, it is easy to conclude that galaxies and stars did not exist before I existed, and it might be as easy to dominate or master them as it is to dominate or master any other ideas of mine. As philosophical realists, however, Marxists should be the last people to claim that humans have or ever will conquer nature in this way.

Now it may surprise some people to learn that Fichte's antirealist view cannot be refuted, any more than the realist view can. There is no final and conclusive argument for either realism or antirealism. Recognizing this, some philosophers simply dismiss the twin questions: "How do I know there is nothing but thoughts and thinkers?" and "How do I know there is something other than thoughts and thinkers?" They argue that since no really satisfactory answer (or, as philosophers put it, no "non-question-begging answer") can be given to either question, in a way they aren't even genuine questions. And if they aren't genuine questions, no one should feel compelled to answer them. Rather, philosophers should aim at curing people of the urge to believe these are questions worth asking in the first place.

Whatever the merit of these arguments, one thing is certain: One cannot accept Fichte's view of things and remain a materialist. Materialists reject claims like life is but a dream or, as the joke goes, there is no problem so bad that suicide won't help. Whatever else materialists may believe, they must be committed to philosophical realism. Unlike many professorial philosophers of his day, Lenin recognized this fact when in his book *Materialism and Empirio-Criticism* he wrote: "the fundamentalist premise of materialism is the recognition of the external world, of the existence of *things* outside and independent of our mind."[4]

As it stands, however, this fundamental premise, taken by itself, is too broad to serve as an all-purpose definition of materialism. For one thing, if we were to classify all realists as materialists, we would have to apply the term *materialist* to people who believe in angels, ghosts, and spirits, as long as these spiritual beings bump into nonspiritual furniture every now and then. And we would also have to apply the term to people who believe in such doctrines as karma and divine judgment.

So it is not enough to be a philosophical realist in order to count as a materialist. To hone down our definition of materialism, we need to consider the second materialist thesis: the claim that thoughts about objects are not the same thing as the objects about which we have thoughts.

Now, it doesn't take too much reflection to persuade oneself that if thoughts have any characteristics at all, they must be different from the characteristics of objects that are not products of activity in someone's brain. After all, as the Dutch philosopher Benedict Spinoza observed, the *idea* of sugar is not sweet, even though the white stuff we put in our tea *is* sweet.

The thesis that thoughts about things are not the same thing as the things about which we have thoughts has an important bearing on the question of what truth is. This might be a good point to take up that question, while at the same time making the second materialist thesis a bit clearer.

If we took another look at our lump of sugar, we might notice that it is white and sweet, but it is not true or false. In fact, no nonlinguistic object is true or false. *Statements* are the only things that can be true or false.[5] Aside from true statements about objects, events, or states of affairs, there is no truth. Furthermore, since any statement must be "in" a language, we can conclude that there is no truth "outside of" one language or another.

Thus, no one who wants to be a consistent materialist can argue that Truth with a capital *T* is something "out there," literally to be discovered like a buried treasure. Truth is not discovered or revealed, because statements are not discovered or revealed. Truth, and hence knowledge, is produced.

Furthermore, because it doesn't make much sense to talk about a language that is the private possession of one person alone, we can say that knowledge is the product of *social* activity. In fact, language and the use of language to produce true and false statements are common to all the activities (or, as we will call them in Chapter 2, the *social practices*) that make up a society.[6]

When we say that geologists are committed to the truth, what we mean is that they are committed to producing true statements about such things as the formation and movement of the earth's crust. Similarly, when we say that Marxists are committed to the truth, what we mean is that they are committed to producing true statements about social relations, exploitation, class conflict, class rule, state power, ideology, and other social realities. Historical materialism enables Marxists who undertake what Lenin called a "concrete analysis of a concrete situation"[7] to produce true statements about these things and processes systematically and in that way to better determine what their interests are and what their course of action should be.

This is why some Marxists have said that the first rule of revolutionary politics is to tell it like it is. So if Marxists are partisans in philosophy or theory—that is, if they take sides on philosophical or theoretical issues at all—then they should be first and foremost partisans on the side of truth.

Before proceeding to the third materialist thesis, let's turn briefly to one more important philosophical question related to the second thesis. This is the question of how we can justify the belief that one statement or another is true. In other words, how can we be sure that we know something?

Some philosophers have suggested that if we were to accept the thesis that knowledge of an object is different from the object itself, we could never be sure that we have knowledge about reality independent of the mind. Of course, if by "reality independent of the mind" these philosophers mean "unknown reality," then it is trivially true that we cannot know it. After all, once we know something it becomes a known reality! So, perhaps in some uninteresting sense of the word *independence*, we cannot know reality that is "independent of mind," any more than we can move an immovable object or resist an irresistible force. (By the same token, we could never know that we don't know it, either!) Conversely, when Marxists discuss reality independent of the mind they do not mean "unknown reality." Rather, they mean "objects and events that exist whether they are known or not."

Let us return to the question of how we can say with justification that a statement is true or false. According to one influential account, we can only know that a statement is true if it is guaranteed by other claims that are at least as certain as the claim in question. To take a well-known example from the seventeenth-century French philosopher René Descartes, the truth of the statement "I exist" is supposed to be guaranteed by the statement "I think," because the second statement taken by itself is supposedly more difficult to doubt than the first one taken by itself.[8] According to this account, then, the sum total of human knowledge can be represented as an upside-down pyramid, resting on at least one belief at the tip. Descartes held that the belief "I think" is at the tip of the pyramid. This belief must either somehow guarantee its own truth or not need any guarantee. Furthermore, every true belief must be connected, directly or indirectly, with the belief at the tip of the pyramid. Thus, for Descartes the belief "I exist," which he believed to follow directly from "I think," is located nearer to the tip of the pyramid than, say, the belief that other people exist, too.

There are a number of problems with this upside-down pyramid picture of knowledge, including the fact that after much searching and more than one false lead, no one (including Descartes) has come up with a belief that really merits being put at the tip of the pyramid. For this and other reasons, the upside-down pyramid picture of knowledge is unsatisfactory.

If we reject this picture, however, then how can we ever be sure that the sciences, including historical materialism, provide accurate statements about actual states of affairs? After all, some philosophers claim that because there is no such thing as an absolutely unshakable belief upon which all the rest of knowledge and science can be built, there can be no such thing as scientific knowledge or, for that matter, any other sort of knowledge.

This is facile, of course. After all, if this claim were true it would be its own counterexample. But how can we know that sciences provide genuine knowledge about actual states of affairs? This leads to an advanced discussion about scientific explanation. To put it briefly, we know that the various sciences provide genuine knowledge about actual objects and events because the sciences are self-correcting enterprises that, taken together, can put any claim in jeopardy, but not all claims at once. The Austrian philosopher Otto Neurath illustrated this point well when he wrote that a science is like a ship that is constantly being rebuilt plank by plank, while it remains afloat on the ocean. I will return to this point later in this chapter.

In the meantime, let's consider the materialist thesis that objects and events in some sense have primacy over knowledge about them. How should we understand this claim?

When Marx, in the passage quoted at the beginning of this chapter, wrote that being determines consciousness, he meant, among other things, that if it were not for the human brain and the processes that take place in the brain, there would be no human thought. Marx contrasted this view to philosophical views that hold that thoughts float around the world like ghosts without any connection to physical things such as brains and yet somehow cause events to happen. We run into more or less sophisticated versions of this last view every day in classrooms, magazines, novels, and television.

Marx also contrasted his view to a view held by some philosophers that in a sense there are two separate worlds—a world of thoughts and an entirely distinct world of things that are not thoughts. For most Marxists, by contrast, there is no good reason to believe that thoughts are located in a different world than things. This view might not sound very surprising, but many philosophers and religious thinkers believe otherwise.

Now, it is pretty obvious that we don't produce food, shelter, and the other things we want and need by simply thinking of them, the way God created Heaven and Earth, according to the biblical book of *Genesis*. In order to get what we want and need, we have to move our arms and hands and put other organs to work in addition to our brains.

Just as the work we do to produce the things we want and need is not limited to our nervous systems alone, this work is not limited to our own individual bodies, either. A carpenter who wants to make a table, for example, will have to take hold of tools and some sort of raw material, such as wood. Producing a table as well as learning, communicating, playing, and even just sitting still require changing things that are already at hand, whether the things changed are wood, metal, plastic, paper, electrical signals, or air waves. Thus, in order to know anything, to cope at all, or to engage in any activity whatsoever, we must transform materials already at hand, materials that are neither part of ourselves nor products of the brain alone. This is another way of putting a point we already mentioned; knowledge is *produced*, not discovered or revealed.

In Chapter 2 we will see that even the carpenter is in a sense a product of society, like the table. Having said this, however, we need to recognize that when Marx claimed that the social being of humans determines their consciousness, he did not necessarily mean that their physical makeup and the various ways they organize themselves in different societies doom people always to think a certain way and no other, the way a billiard ball takes one course and no other when struck in a specific way by a pool cue. True, in an important sense our physical makeup and the sort of society in which we live determine the way we think; however, thinking also changes society. After all, to take an example close at hand, the life works of Marx and Engels have clearly had a great influence on recent history. Indeed, if thinking does not change society, then it is a waste of time for Marxists to study Marxist theory.

Just as knowledge requires the transformation of material, it also bears the marks of the manner in which production, distribution, exchange, and consumption of goods take place in a particular society. In capitalist societies, for example, some of the most widespread scientific conclusions are those that have proven useful in reducing the cost of producing goods for the market and, thus, (in the short term at least) in increasing the rate of profit for a capitalist. This might be one reason why mathematics and physics are so uncontroversial in capitalist societies. Conversely, if a scientific field has no obvious use to a ruling class, and if it represents a possible threat to existing class relations, it may be suppressed. This was how high church officials viewed Galileo's conclusions in his day, and it is how capitalists view historical materialism today.

But even when members of a ruling class view a science as valuable, the conclusions of that science might not be widely accepted outside of a small circle of specialists. In fact, even (or perhaps especially) in the richest and most technologically advanced capitalist countries today, there are plenty of people, including specialists in the sciences, who do not accept the conclusions reached by the sciences.

This last point becomes more understandable after a tour of the so-called "social science" departments of large universities in the West. These departments are fragmented into various specialized fields, such as "mainstream" economics, sociology, history, anthropology, political science, and so on. Social scientists in these universities have developed supersophisticated techniques such as econometrics, game theory, and various complicated models and methods of research. Nevertheless, in their hands, these techniques, models, and methods produce at best shallow descriptions of narrowly conceived problems. Furthermore, these social scientists typically have little understanding of the history of their disciplines or of alternative approaches outside the mainstream of officially approved doctrines. As a result, they are unlikely ever to "see the forest for the trees." And even when researchers from a number of different disciplines meet to share their views, they bring with them their officially approved assumptions and departmental divisions.

This is why so many interdisciplinary meetings have just repeated over and over again the stale claims of the past.

In the remaining chapters I hope to make the point that Marx took a very different approach to the study of history and society. He resisted oversimplification and insisted on a detailed and deep "concrete analysis of a concrete situation," as Lenin put it. At the same time, however, he also summed up these analyses and, where possible, drew connections. Following his example, historical materialists defy the conventional division of the social sciences into economics, sociology, anthropology, political science, and so on.

Marxism Differs from Other Forms of Materialism

Marx, then, was a materialist. But he was not just any sort of materialist. For one thing, unlike many materialists of the past, he emphasized the fact that what he studied constantly changes. For Marx, the study of society was the study of social change. As we shall see in Chapter 2, societies have changed radically over the centuries. It is essential, then, that we should recognize change when it takes place and not approach things as if they were eternally fixed, or as if all change were just tick-tock repetition, like the swinging of a pendulum. In this respect, Marx was about as far as one can get from the writers who claim that history itself has come to an end along with the Cold War.

It is also important to recognize that when things change they do not always do so in a simple and smooth manner. For long periods of time it sometimes seems as though there is nothing new, and the only changes that take place are reruns of what has happened in the past or a smooth increase or decrease of a particular quality in a thing. There are, of course, changes of this kind: When heated, water gradually increases in temperature, and when cooled, its temperature decreases one degree at a time. As we know, however, this sort of smooth increase or decrease leads sooner or later to a rapid and complete change in water's most important characteristics. Marxists have traditionally called this stage of change *the transformation of quantity into quality*. At the freezing or boiling point, water suddenly changes from liquid into solid or gas, respectively. Similarly, societies change radically, even though for many long years it can seem that we have only an endless swinging back and forth between two governing parties, or liberal and conservative political forces, both committed to extending ruling-class rule forever into the future.

By keeping in mind that things always change and that change is often uneven and sometimes explosive, it is easier to notice trends that might otherwise be overlooked and to demand explanations when others don't see the need for them. In the following chapters we will see that societies have changed radically over the centuries and that capitalism is a fundamentally different social arrangement from what came before. As simple as this may sound, many "social scientists" in Western universities do not acknowledge it to be the case. By failing to recognize that fundamental social change has in fact taken place and will continue to take place, they excuse themselves from the task of trying to explain how and why this is so.

So far we have encountered two general conclusions drawn from a wide range of observations. (1) When studying something, be aware that it has a history and is still undergoing change and be ready to recognize further change. (2) Be aware that change is not always gradual or quantitative: Sometimes quantitative change leads to explosive or qualitative change in the object or process studied. These two general conclusions can be restated as methodological principles, or very general principles to guide research. (In Chapter 2, we will discuss a third principle, according to which things we study should be viewed as what some Marxists call *unities of opposites*.)

Marxists have traditionally called these methodological principles laws of materialist dialectics. These laws are so general that they appear to apply not only to historical materialism but to other scientific fields as well. Researchers in the branch of physics called cosmology, for example, believe they can at least partially reconstruct the history of space and time itself—things that not so long ago were assumed by almost everyone to be eternal and unchanging. Similarly, Darwin showed not only that plant and animal species have a history but that the qualitative distinctions among species followed long periods of gradual change and, in turn, that species that exist today are undergoing gradual change.

Some people have criticized Marxists who emphasize materialist dialectics, saying that its principles are so elementary they should go without saying. Unfortunately, however, the prejudice that as it was in the past, so shall it always be is very common and deeply ingrained. This is why we constantly need to remind ourselves that things change, and that, from time to time, change takes place as an explosion, a leap, a qualitative change, a revolution.

One of the things that makes Marxist materialism different from other forms of materialism, then, is the dialectical emphasis on change, including uneven and explosive change. I will touch on dialectics again in Chapter 2, when I discuss what it means to view society as a structure. In the meantime, however, students should be warned that, as useful as they are, neither materialist dialectics nor any other methodological principles or rules of thumb are substitutes for deep, detailed research of well-defined problems.

Objections to the View that Marxism Is Scientific

In the past, Soviet philosophers have insisted that Marxists should believe claims such as: There is one basic substance, namely matter, and everything that exists is matter, or all mental processes so far examined are products of material processes, therefore everything mental is a product of material processes. Seizing on these sorts of claims, some philosophers in the West have portrayed Marxism as being based on shaky speculations or metaphysics. Time and again, however, Marx and Lenin made it clear that they did not believe it was the job of philosophers to go about discovering basic substances for physicists.

More serious objections have been raised against Marxism by a school of philosophy called *positivism*. According to the positivists, genuinely scientific theories must include laws that we can use to predict future events the way an astronomer, for example, can use Isaac Newton's laws of motion to predict the next time a comet will pass near Earth. Marx's theory, by contrast, does not allow us to do anything of the kind. We cannot plug economic statistics into Marx's theory and then crank out a forecast of social change. It is true that some Marxists have spoken as though this were possible if we only had enough information. They thought that just as Newton had discovered laws of motion for stars and planets, Marx had discovered iron laws that enable us to predict the future course of history. So far, however, these particular Marxists have failed to show that such predictions can be made, even under the most favorable conditions. Since historical materialism has not allowed us to test its accuracy by predicting social change with precision, some postivists have claimed that it is not a science and could never be one.

It is not necessary, however, for every field of study to conform to the picture of physics in order to rate as a genuine science. Darwin's theory of natural selection provides no laws that we can use to predict the appearance of a new species of plant the way an astronomer can predict the return of a comet. This is one reason why positivist opponents of Marxism, like the English philosopher Karl Popper, have also denied that evolutionary biology is a genuinely scientific theory.

Neither Darwin nor Marx founded theories that predict future events the way physicists do. However, the fact that so-called "historical sciences" such as evolutionary biology, geology, or historical materialism do not enable us to make predictions does not prevent us from recognizing these fields as genuine sciences. After all, each of these fields accurately describes underlying causes bringing about changes, whether these changes be the origin of new species, movements of the earth's crust, or social transformations.

Since their heyday in the 1920s, positivists' notions of what a theory must do in order to count as a genuine science have lost favor with most philosophers of science. Actually, to their credit, some of the leading positivists came to recognize how unsatisfactory positivism was, and they themselves led the assault on it. Otto Neurath, whom we met briefly in the previous section, was one such positivist. In spite of the fact that he was a leading positivist, his view of the sciences as ships at sea under constant reconstruction and his criticism of any sharp division between theory and observation tended to undermine the positivist notion of what a theory must do in order to rank as a science.

Even in the West, positivism has been abandoned by many philosophers of science. In spite of this, however, practicing scientists and laypeople continue to subscribe to old positivist assumptions. And people still attack both Marx and Darwin by invoking positivist assumptions about what science is.

Other critics have claimed that historical materialism is not a science now, although it might someday rank as a science, after more work has been done to "fill it out." These people, however, have missed the point that Neurath was trying to make with his picture of the ship: No science is complete or provides infallible answers to all the questions that can be raised about its object of study. Religious doctrines and metaphysical systems claim to be able to answer all such questions. What makes a science a science, by contrast, is that it continues to provide new knowledge about some sort of object, new descriptions of causes of change, whether they be the movement of planets and stars, the combination of chemical elements, the origin of new species of animals, or the appearance of new social systems.

Early in his career, Lenin wrote: "We most certainly do not look upon the theory of Marx as something permanent and immutable; on the contrary, we remain convinced that it has merely laid the foundation stone of the science which socialists must advance in all directions if they want to keep abreast of life."[9]

By contrast, the orthodox Marxists, who portray Marxism as a doctrine that is complete in every one of its details, undermine their own claims that historical materialism is a science.

Furthermore, it is also an error to claim that historical materialism cannot be a science because its founders were mistaken on one point or another. After all, it would certainly be unfair to reject evolutionary biology by arguing against the opinion of Charles Darwin's predecessor Jean-Baptiste Lamarck that traits animals acquire after birth are passed on to the next generation. Rejection of evolutionary biology on the basis of Lamarck's opinion would be unfair even though there are enough passages in Darwin's masterpiece, *The Origin of Species*, to show that Darwin did in fact accept Lamarck's erroneous opinion on this matter. Nonetheless, Darwin is justly credited with having founded the new science of evolutionary biology, because he identified irreversible change where earlier researchers had noticed only slight variations from a stable state of affairs. It is here that Darwin demonstrated his originality, and it is here that we can locate the break between Darwin and his prescientific predecessors.

In the same way, what interests us about Marx is not this or that idea or turn of phrase he borrowed from predecessors like the idealist philosopher G.W.F. Hegel or the economist David Ricardo. What interests us about Marx is the way in which he broke away from the assumptions of his predecessors, rejecting not just their conclusions but the very terms of their arguments.

Marx's great achievement lies in his conception of human history as a part of natural history. Just as Darwin "historicized nature" by showing that species change and new species arise as old ones disappear, Marx "naturalized history" by showing that historical and social change can be explained without resorting to supernatural agencies, whether they be gods or "invisible hands."

Summary

Key terms discussed in this chapter include *philosophical realism, idealist philosophy* (or *idealism*), *materialism, historical materialism, dialectics, the transformation of quantity into quality,* and *positivism*.

Marxist theory is made up of several fields of study, which, in the interpretation presented in this primer, nevertheless constitute one coherent body of thought: historical materialism, the materialist conception of history.

As materialists, Marxists hold that: (1) There are things other than thoughts and thinkers, (2) knowledge of something is different from the actual thing known, and (3) objects and events in some sense have primacy over knowledge about them.

Marxists reject Descartes's picture of all knowledge and science as an upside-down pyramid resting on one absolutely certain belief. The Marxist view is closer to Otto Neurath's picture of a ship of connected scientific beliefs gradually being rebuilt plank by plank while remaining afloat on the ocean.

One way in which Marxists differ from other materialists is that they stress the importance of change—usually gradual or quantitative, but sometimes rapid, explosive, or qualitative.

So far, at least, Marxism has not enabled us to predict the future course of social change the way astronomers predict the future course of planets. In spite of this, however, historical materialism is a genuine science, because it is consistent with materialism, and it is an open-ended and self-correcting enterprise that provides adequate explanations of why societies are as they are and why social transformations take place.

Reading List

Engels, Friederich. *Ludwig Feuerbach and the Outcome of Classical German Philosophy*. New York: International Publishers, 1934. An account of how far Marx grew away from the philosophical tradition in which he was trained as a young man. The distinction Engels makes in this book between a philosophical method and a philosophical system, however, is not very useful.

———. "Speech at the Graveside of Karl Marx." Engels's tribute, delivered on March 17, 1883, appears in a number of anthologies, including Robert C. Tucker (ed.) *The Marx-Engels Reader* (New York: W. W. Norton & Co., 1972), pp. 603–604.

*Gramsci, Antonio. "The Study of Philosophy," in *Selections from the Prison Notebooks*. New York: International Publishers, 1971, pp. 323–377. Gramsci made the point that "the majority of mankind are philosophers." What is less certain, however, is Gramsci's view that one can judge how rational a way of thinking is by determining whether or not masses of people subscribe to it (refer to *Prison Notebooks*, p. 341).

Lenin, V.I. *Materialism and Empirio-Criticism*. Moscow: Progress Publishers, 1970. Lenin did not write this book as a professional philosopher but as a "rank-and-file Marxist." It should not come as a surprise, then, that professional philosophers in the West have not thought much of the book. Nevertheless, as the English philosopher Anthony Flew pointed out in his book *Philosophy: An Introduction* (Buffalo, N.Y.: Prometheus Books, 1980, p. 70), the book contains important insights for which Lenin has not been given full credit in the West.

_____. "On the Question of Dialectics" (included in Lenin's *Collected Works*, vol. 38). These suggestive remarks, which Lenin jotted down in 1915, focus on "the unity of opposites"—a topic we will take up in Chapter 2.

*Marx, Karl. *Theses on Feuerbach*. Included in David McLellan, ed., *Karl Marx: Selected Writings* (Oxford: Oxford University Press, 1977), pp. 156–158. Notes to himself, not intended for publication, but published by Engels after Marx's death. These eleven points are difficult to understand, but they offer insight into Marx's departure from the philosophical traditions of his day.

*Karl Marx
(1818–1883)*

*Friedrich Engels
(1820–1895)*

Founders of Historical Materialism

Next to almost anyone else, Friedrich Engels would have stood alone as a great and original thinker. It is a tribute to his modesty that he devoted so much of himself to his comrade and friend, Karl Marx. According to Marx, Engels's early essay *The Condition of the Working Class in England* convinced him of the need to study economics carefully. From 1844 until Marx's death, the two men shared ideas, encouraged each other and together worked out the broad outlines of historical materialism. Later in life, Engels helped to support Marx and his family, and after Marx's death Engels set aside his own work to prepare his friend's unfinished writings for publication.

Marx spent nearly twenty years in the British Museum in London researching his lifework, *Capital*, the first volume of which was published in 1867. *Capital* is more than a painstakingly detailed study of capitalism in England in the nineteenth century. The work is also a powerful critique of the dominant ideas of the capitalist class—ideas about "Man," "History" and "the Wealth of Nations." But even more important, *Capital* provides a broad framework for explaining social change over the long sweep of history.

Marx and Engels were not just thinkers, though. During the revolutionary upheaval in Germany in 1848, Engels fought on the barricades and manned artillery. Marx, for his part, was hounded by censors, ordered arrested for high treason, banished from Paris, and forced to renounce his German citizenship. He and his family lived the rest of their lives in exile, mostly in London, where they settled in 1849. In 1864, Marx and Engels helped to found the International Workingmen's Association (the so-called First International) in London, and for years after that Marx was an active member of the association's general council. In 1889 Engels also took part in founding the Second International.

By far their most important contribution to workers' movements, however, was their lifetime theoretical work. In 1867, as Marx finished the first volume of *Capital,* he wrote to a friend in the United States:

> I had to use every moment in which I was capable of work in order that I might finish the task to which I had sacrificed my health, my happiness in life and my family . . . I laugh at the so-called "practical" men and their wisdom. If one chose to be an ox one could, of course, turn one's back on the agonies of mankind and look after one's own skin. But I should really have regarded myself as *impractical* if I had departed without completely finishing my book at least in manuscript.[10]

Franz Mehring's biography, *Karl Marx: The Story of His Life,* is both a classic of Marxism and a literary classic. The book was first published in Germany in 1918; an English translation was published by the University of Michigan Press in 1962. Gustav Mayer's book, *Friedrich Engels: A Biography* (New York, A. A. Knopf, 1936), is an equally outstanding biography of Marx's friend and comrade.

Notes

1. David McLellan, ed., *Karl Marx: Selected Writings* (Oxford: Oxford University Press, 1977), p. 225.

2. Karl Marx, *Capital* Vol. 1 (New York: International Publishers, 1967), p. 10.

3. Friedrich Engels, *Anti-Duhring* (New York: International Publishers, 1939), p. 285.

4. V.I. Lenin, *Materialism and Empirio-Criticism* (Moscow: Progress Publishers, 1970), p. 70.

5. Of course, we sometimes describe a person, an arrow, or something else as being "true," but in such cases we are using the word as a synonym for "honest," "genuine," or "accurately aimed."

6. At the same time, we need to emphasize an unsurprising point we have already hinted at in discussing the first materialist thesis: Society is not composed only of language. Both of these points will become clearer in the next chapter.

7. V.I. Lenin, *Collected Works* Vol. 3 (Moscow: Progress Publishers, 1966), p. 166.

8. Descartes's argument appears in his *Meditations on First Philosophy*, first published in 1641.

9. V.I. Lenin, *Collected Works* Vol. 4 (Moscow: Progress Publishers, 1977), p. 184.

10. Karl Marx, Letter of April 30, 1867, reprinted in Saul K. Padover (ed.), *The Letters of Karl Marx* (Englewood Cliffs, N.J.: Prentice-Hall, 1979), pp. 228–229.

2

What Is a Society?

But the human essence is no abstraction inherent in each single individual. In its reality it is the ensemble of social relations.

—*Karl Marx*

In Chapter 1, I suggested that historical materialism is a genuinely scientific study of society and social change. But what is a society? In order to answer this question, we will need to identify the main parts of a society and then consider how they are related. This chapter is a broad overview of the main parts, aspects, or dimensions of a society. Once we have in view what a society is in broad outline, we will turn to the Marxist analysis of capitalist society in Chapters 3 and 4.

Many of us have heard some version of the following story: Long ago, people realized they could better pursue their own individual interests by living together and accepting certain limits on their behavior than by living like lone wolves in the forest. Thus, for instance, the miller realized that by paying the farmer a fair price for his grain, he need no longer divide his attention between growing his own grain and milling it into flour. And by selling his flour to a broker at a fair price, the miller need not worry about lugging it all to the retail market. The situation is similar in the case of the baker, the grocer, and the buyer of bread. Thus, every member of a society benefits by associating, as long as everyone abides by standards of fairness and legality.

All of this may sound rather obvious and not worth arguing about. Nevertheless, this account of how societies originated is based on a number of shaky assumptions that the founders of historical materialism rejected. We will discuss two of these assumptions in the next section. By the end of the section it should be clear that when at least some Marxists use the word *society*, they mean something very differ-

27

ent from what many other people mean. In fact, some Marxists prefer to use the term *social formation*, to avoid confusion.

Society as a Structure Made Up of Practices

First of all, Marxists do not view society as something that was created one fine day long ago, when lone individuals came together after realizing they had a common interest in pursuing their individual aims in association with others. For one thing, this story flies in the face of a lot of evidence that, with rare exceptions, humans have always lived together in one sort of social group or another. More importantly, however, the story conflicts with the fact that in order for a group of people to voluntarily associate, they must already have a good deal in common. Among other things, for example, they must be able to communicate in some way, so they must already have a language in common, however simple it may be. Thus, "individuals" who are lone wolves at heart could never come together to form a society in the first place.

This objection underscores the Marxist view that a society is not a simple grouping of self-contained individuals, as if people were ready-made bricks, and all the different societies from prehistoric times to the present day were just piles of these bricks stacked in different ways. Indeed, as we will see in this chapter, it would be more accurate to say that individuals are the products of societies, rather than vice versa.

But if individual people are not the building blocks of a society, then what are the main parts of a society that we should study in order to understand it? The Marxist answer to this question is that a society, viewed as a whole, is a unity of various processes of production, or practices. Before going on to explain this answer, however, we need to prepare the ground by introducing several new terms.

"Man" certainly does not live by bread alone. Nevertheless, it is just as certain that humans cannot live without bread or some other source of nutrition. Bread and other things that members of a society need or want are said to have value as useful objects, or to be *use-values*. The usefulness of bread is its nutritional content and perhaps also its pleasant taste, whereas the usefulness of perfume, presumably, is its nice smell. Some use-values, such as food, clothing, shelter, and heating fuel, are means of subsistence, or things that people want because without them it would be difficult to survive. Others, such as perfume or alcohol, are not means of subsistence. Marx recognized the difference between these two sorts of "wants," but he also noted that "the nature of such wants, whether, for instance, they spring from the stomach or from fancy, makes no difference"[1] for economists.

Now, there would be no bread without seed, soil, water, and sunlight, of course. By the same token, however, all the seed, soil, water, and sunlight in the world will never result in bread unless the seed is sown, the grain is reaped and milled into flour, the flour is mixed with water and made into dough, and the dough is baked. Productive activity, or *labor*, is necessary in order to change natural resources like soil, water, and sunlight into bread and other natural resources into perfume and other things we find useful, or use-values. (Some use-values, of course, including the air we breath, are already at hand without the intervention of labor.)

Once natural resources are affected by labor, they become raw materials. With a few exceptions that prove the rule, things that are bought and sold have had some amount of labor time expended on them.[2] Diamonds in the rough, for example, are raw materials because they have been mined.

A raw material or anything else that people need or want is a *good*. Bread, alcohol, automobiles, cultivated land, and innumerable other things we come into contact with every day are goods. Many goods are produced—that is, they are the result in part of an expenditure of human energy; they are products of labor. Other goods, such as fresh air, water, and sunlight, are not products of labor (so far at least!).

It is important to keep in mind that labor is not the only source of wealth. No economic production could take place without raw materials and hence natural resources. Marx emphasized this point when in *Capital*, volume 1, he quoted the seventeenth-century English political economist William Petty, who wrote, with reference to national wealth, that "labor is its father and the earth its mother."[3]

Returning to the main topic of this section, we may now advance the following point: Many (though not all, as we shall see) of the most important *social practices* are processes involving laborers changing raw materials into products by means of certain tools, skills, and knowledge. In a sugar refinery, for example, trained workers who are organized in a certain way expend their energy operating various machines to transform raw cane or beet into some form of sugar. In this example it is easy to identify four sorts of things without which many social practices cannot take place: (1) a certain sort of labor, (2) a certain sort of raw material that is already at hand, (3) certain instruments of production (including tools, machinery, and factory buildings) as well as certain skills, knowledge, and forms of organization that are already at hand, and (4) a certain result, or product.

Refining sugar, of course, is only one process among innumerable others that make up a larger social practice of producing goods and services. Taken as a whole, all of the processes of producing, distributing, and exchanging goods and services in a society make up the economic structure, or the economic practice of that society.

Lenin once described Marxist theory as the science dealing with the development of historical systems of social production. This is a good definition. It is important to stress, however, that economic production is never the only sort of production that takes place in a society. In the societies in which we live, for example, many things besides goods are produced from day to day. These include such "things" as the rule of law, political authority, and religious rituals. It may sound strange to think of these as products, but they are all literally results of certain sorts of labor applied to certain preexisting materials, using certain "tools." In capitalist societies today, for example, the rule of law is reproduced from day to day and from moment to moment, thanks to "police work," massive public relations campaigns, surveillance and crowd control techniques, tear gas, shotguns, prisons, and courts of law. The moment this process of production (or more accurately, *re*-production) breaks down, as it sometimes does, the rule of law is no longer in effect. The situation is similar in the cases of political authority, religious rituals, morality, and art. In this sense, then, the rule of law, political authority, religion, morality, art, and other ideological and political activities are all products of noneconomic social practices.

We can say, then, that political and ideological activities are just as much parts of social production as economic activities are. Political and ideological practices differ from economic production, however, because the results of the former practices are not goods. In Chapter 3 we'll take a somewhat closer look at economic practice in capitalist societies, and in Chapter 4 we'll turn our attention briefly to political and ideological practices in capitalist societies.

In the meantime, we should register the following point: If we survey a wide range of societies, we can identify at least two main sorts of social practices: economic practice and ideological practice. Any society, taken as a whole, is a unity of these two sorts of practices, among others. As we'll see in the next section, political practice arose when societies appeared that were divided along class lines.

Some very important social activities that are not clearly productive include such personal relations as child-rearing, the care of old people and the sick, sexual relations, and friendships. It is easy to see, however, that these activities are inseparable from economic and ideological practices and that productive relations to a large extent determine the sort of family relations, sexual relations, and friendships that are characteristic of a given society.

In Chapter 1, I hinted that scientific knowledge is also a result of a social process of production. Knowledge doesn't just pop up out of thin air, any more than bread does. In order to produce scientific knowledge, "brain power" must be expended to transform a "raw material" (the notions and true and false beliefs that we might think of as some of the planks on Neurath's ship) into knowledge by using certain concepts, theories, skills, and other "tools" already at hand.

As I mentioned earlier, in order to understand what a society is, it is not enough just to identify its parts. We also need to understand how those parts are related to each other within a society as a whole. In the rest of this section, I will explain what Marxists mean when they say that society, viewed as a whole, is a *structure* of practices.

To begin, let's consider a fisherman's net as a sort of structure. A net is not just a pile of string. Every single cord of a net is directly or indirectly connected to every other cord. So when a fish swims into a net, it displaces every one of the net's cords to one degree or another, depending on the location of the fish in relation to each cord of the net as a whole. In the same way, as we have seen, a society is not simply a collection of individual members. And it is not just a collection of institutions or activities. What makes a society what it is are the ways in which food, shelter, information, art, and so on are produced, distributed, exchanged, and consumed. Like cords in a net, every social practice is directly or indirectly related to every other practice. For example, we'll see in Chapter 4 how important political practice is to economic production. So it is the relationship of practices to each other that makes a society what it is.

It is important to keep in mind that there is nothing sacred or eternal about the particular social practices that exist today, or about the way they are related to each other. True, economic practices take place in all societies. Every materialist recognizes this. At the same time, Marxists recognize that no societies are made up solely of economic practices. Nevertheless, as we will see in later chapters, for example, societies without classes lacked the dimension of political practice that is so important to the societies in which we live today. Furthermore, in some feudal societies, religious ideological practices were much more important in relation to political practice than they are in most societies today. Or to take another example, the production of scientific knowledge is so highly developed today that scientific activity can be thought of as an important social practice in its own right, inseparable but distinct from economic and ideological practices. As these examples indicate, then, even the barest, most general features of a social structure differ from one case to the next and from century to century.

In the case of a net, each cord can bear about as much weight as any other cord. So in this sense each cord of a net is roughly equal to each other cord. A society, by contrast, is a structure made up of parts that are very unequal, as far as determining the character of the structure as a whole is concerned. For example, one characteristic of historical materialism is the claim that, in the final analysis, economic practice carries the most weight when it comes to determining the overall character of a society. This is why we need to examine the economic practice of a society carefully in order to understand social change.

Having said this, however, we should not conclude that the whole character of a society is defined solely by economic practice. It is true that in his preface to *A Critique of Political Economy* (1859) and elsewhere, Marx spoke of the economic structure as the "real foundation" of a society, upon which correspond a "legal and political superstructure" and "definite forms of consciousness."[4] Unfortunately, many writers—including both orthodox Marxists and many opponents of Marxism—have focused on these passages and taken Marx's picture literally. They seem to have forgotten that the terms *economic structure* and *political and ideological superstructure* are metaphors. Marx did not intend them to be taken literally. The point of the metaphor is that the superstructure—including political and ideological practices—could not stay up without the base, or economic practice. As a result, when the dominant economic status of a social group is undermined, the stage is set for a political confrontation, and sometimes social revolution. This is exactly what happened to bring capitalists to political power in England's "Glorious Revolution" of 1640, the French Revolution of 1789, and many other cases.

Without a corresponding economic practice, then, the other practices would fall. Since Marx's death, this view of the importance of economic production in determining the character of a society has come to be widely accepted even by "mainstream social scientists," who would never admit to accepting Marx's thesis that being determines consciousness. At the same time, however, we need to keep in mind that in class societies political and ideological practices play the indispensable role of stabilizing economic practice the way a tabletop stabilizes the legs that hold it up. This is the best way of viewing Marx's metaphor of the superstructure and the economic base. This point should become clearer when we investigate the relationships between economic, political, and ideological practices in Chapter 4.

Modes of Production

Instruments of production plus the natural resources at hand, together with the people who operate them and the acquired skill and know-how of these people make up the *productive forces* in a society. The productive forces, then, consist of the work force, together with natural resources, tools, techniques, and knowledge by which humans make materials usable. So the productive forces are that part of a process of production that includes the relations of people to the objects and forces of nonhuman nature they use to produce their food, clothing, shelter, and other necessities and luxuries for living.

In the course of economic production, however, humans act not only on nonhuman objects but also on one another. In order to produce goods, humans enter into definite connections and relations with one another. Only within these social relations does production take place. Some of these social relations are cooperative and do not involve domination and control. Others are established by custom or law and are enforced either by members of the society as a whole or by a special section of society that we will call the *state*, which we will discuss later. The relations of people and social groups to one another during the course of economic production, distribution, and exchange make up the relations of economic production of a society. For convenience, Marxists refer to the relations of economic production as simply *relations of production* or *productive relations*.

Thus, there are two aspects of economic practice: the technical aspect of natural resources, tools, and skills and the interpersonal level of cooperation, exchange, authority, and control.

We can get an idea of the variety of relations of production that have existed by gaining an overview of different sorts of societies.

Within so-called "primitive" societies, for instance, all able-bodied members of the tribe or clan worked together hunting, fishing, gathering fruits, vegetables, and roots, raising the children, and so on, and they all divided everything up among themselves. In ancient Egypt, Greece, and Rome, conversely, slaves engaged in economic production, while slave owners received the whole product minus what was necessary to sustain the slave and perhaps to ensure the existence of a future generation of slaves. In the Middle Ages in Europe, separate peasant households usually worked individual plots of land on their lords' estates. Their lords, in turn, expected from them either a part of each household's small plot harvest, or taxes in the form of money, or work for part of the year on the landowners' fields. In the capitalist societies in which we live today, by contrast, the tasks that most workers perform typically make them much more dependent on other workers. At the same time, workers go to factories and offices that they do not own and work with tools, machines, and raw materials owned by others.

We will return to the question of capitalist relations of production in Chapter 3. In the meantime, as the overview in the previous paragraph suggests, the state of the relations of production in a society furnishes the answer to the question: Who controls the *means of production*—the land, forests, waters, mineral resources, raw materials, instruments of production, production sites, plants, factories, computers, offices, means of transportation, communication, information storage and retrieval, and so on? (The means of production consist of instruments of production together with raw materials.)

Let's recall the conclusion drawn earlier in this chapter, that a society is a unity of various social practices of production, not just economic practice. Broadly speaking, then, many of the relations among members of a society and social groups are productive relations.[5] Marx emphasized this point when he wrote that society is made up of the productive relations *in their totality*. Now, if we were to ignore the Marxist view that the phrase *productive relations in their totality* includes social relations of ideological production, political practice, and other sorts of practices, then we would arrive at the sort of crude caricature that some opponents of Marxism are so fond of knocking over.

Keeping in mind our earlier conclusions, then, we can think of a society as a field or network of social relations and of each member of a society as occupying a certain position, station, or location within this field. Once we register this fact, it follows that human beings are what they are and do what they do not just by virtue of being members of a certain species of animal but also by virtue of the positions they occupy within a given social field, or society. Every human being must eat in order to survive; nevertheless, as Marx noted, one sort of human eats raw meat with tooth and nail, whereas others eat cooked food with a fork and knife. So when Marxists talk about social relations they do not mean relations among ready-made individuals. Rather, social relations themselves have a major hand in determining the character of the members of a society who are related to one another. In other words, every member of a society is in large part determined by what Marx, in his Sixth Thesis on Feuerbach, called "the ensemble of social relations."[6]

A close examination of a wide variety of different societies will confirm the following observation: Certain productive forces together with certain relations of production make up a number of identifiable systems of production, or what Marxists call *modes of production*. Let's take a quick look at how various modes of production have arisen.

Many of us have been brought up assuming that societies have always been divided into "haves" and "have-nots." This, however, is not accurate. Not only have there been egalitarian, communal societies but if, as most researchers agree today, our species has existed more or less in its present form for at least 100,000 years, then societies divided into classes of "haves" and "have-nots" have only been around for at most 7 percent of the time humans have existed.

There has been a great variety of communal societies. What they all had in common, however, was collective ownership by all members of society of everything except items of personal use such as clothes, tools, and such. All members of communal societies except perhaps the very young and the very old probably had to work a long time to gather or produce food, shelter, and the other things necessary for the group to survive. Nevertheless, we would not be justified in concluding from this that life in communal societies was uniformly "savage." In the nineteenth century, among the Iroquois Indians of North America, for example, the tribes arrived at important decisions collectively, the youngest members of the tribes were treated with kindness, women had much influence on collective decisionmaking, and members of a tribe had greater opportunities for choice and diversity than did the European settlers who considered the Iroquois to be savages.

There is no iron law that dictates that a communal society ever *has to* develop into anything else. The Aborigines of Australia, for example, existed for thousands of years without ever becoming slave owners or slaves. What's more, some communal societies still exist today in the Amazon Basin, Southeast Asia, sub-Saharan Africa, and elsewhere. The fact remains, however, that many communal societies did change into societies based on slave ownership and slave labor. Starting perhaps seven or eight thousand years ago, there appeared communities that sowed seed and raised domesticated animals on land they shared in common. These and other innovations raised the *productivity of labor*—that is, they enabled humans to produce more from, say, an hour of labor than was possible in centuries past. Irrigated crops bear more fruit than crops that are not irrigated, dams save harvests from flooding, domesticated cattle are a ready source of animal protein that can be regulated in anticipation of lean times.

Not only did these innovations make labor more productive but they also made economic production more complicated. In order to produce metal-tipped plows, for example, some members of a society had to learn special metalworking skills. The more complicated production became, the sharper the distinction became between members of a tribe or clan involved in agricultural production on the one hand and members involved in metalworking, weaving, basket-making, pottery, and other sorts of craft production on the other. Thus, some societies developed a more and more complicated division of labor.

As new tools, crafts, and methods of farming made labor more productive, some goods could be produced not just to be consumed on the spot but to be exchanged with other tribes nearby. An inland tribe could trade, say, their surplus animal skins for the surplus fish oil of a coastal tribe. Eventually, goods began to be produced especially for the purpose of being traded. *Commodity production* is the term for the process whereby goods are produced not to be consumed on the spot but for exchange. The development of commodity production also resulted in a further division of labor among different communal societies.

Before it was possible to produce a social surplus, captives from wars were either killed or adopted as members of the tribe. Since captives could not be put to work to produce more than what was necessary for their own upkeep, it made no sense to keep them as slaves. Once it became possible to produce a social surplus reliably, however, captives could be put to use to increase production further and further beyond what the society needed to survive. This enabled a larger number of noncaptives to live off the work of others and refrain from productive work themselves. What the captives produced beyond what was necessary to keep them alive was taken, or appropriated, by the noncaptives who owned them. Thus there appeared for the first time a division in society between owners who do not work and workers who do not own. *Exploitation* occurs when a surplus product is appropriated from those who produce it by a part of society that does not produce it.

There are different forms of exploitation, each one characteristic of a particular mode of production. In the remainder of this section I would like to say a few words about exploitation in societies that are not capitalist. We will turn to exploitation in capitalist societies in Chapter 3.

With the appearance of slavery, a section of society, the slave owners, no longer had to spend every waking hour producing means of subsistence. They were free to engage in other, less muscular activities. In this way, the relatively simple division of labor that had existed in communal societies became much more complex. No longer was there a division of labor based only on age (very young and very old members of communal societies could not perform the same tasks as other members) and gender (among their other tasks, women had to bear children) or between agriculture and handicrafts. Now there was a new and far-reaching division between the hard manual labor of the slaves on the one hand and the less muscular, more "brainy" work of the slave-masters on the other.

At the same time, the slave owners faced a new problem of large-scale social control. Slave owners had to ensure that their slaves would work and that they would not escape or come together to revolt. This made a new division of labor necessary, since as the slave population grew, so did the need for specialized forces of social control.

Even from this sketchy account it is easy to see how slave owners became the rulers of the earliest states and how, as their methods of rule became more organized, these states grew more complex. In Chapter 4 it will become clear that the states that form a part of the societies in which we live today do essentially the same thing as the simplest slave states: They unify and organize the ruling class of exploiters, and they split and disorganize the various other classes.

As small-scale production developed on a larger and larger scale, slavery as a system became impractical.[7] For one thing, large-scale production brought more slaves into contact with each other, thus making slave revolts more frequent and devastating. The frequent and devastating slave revolts in ancient Rome testify to the potential danger that threatened the slaveholding class. Furthermore, in some slave societies, such as ancient Rome in its later days, serfdom of a sort had already somewhat replaced slave labor in agriculture and handicrafts on the estates of wealthy landowners. (This, by the way, is an example of the coexistence of modes of production within a society, about which I will say a few words in a moment.) For these and other reasons, empires built on slave labor were weakened from inside and open to attack from the outside. In the well-known case of Rome, this combination of internal weaknesses and external threats resulted in the collapse of the empire and the rise of a new sort of society characterized by a new mode of production called feudalism.

The form of exploitation characteristic of feudalism was very different from slavery. Under feudalism, those who produced the social surplus were no longer the private property of those who exploited them; feudal lords did not have the power of life or death over their serfs that slave owners had over their slaves. Nevertheless, serfs were not free to leave the feudal estates where they lived; they were tied to their rulers' land, or estates, by bonds of legal obligation. Feudal serfs in medieval Europe, the Middle East, parts of Africa, and elsewhere cultivated plots of land, which provided a living for themselves and their households. Insofar as they worked for themselves, they had an incentive to increase production. Nevertheless, serfs also had to work on their lords' fields for a certain amount of time each year, or to deliver a certain portion of the harvest of the plot they worked to the lord, or to pay an amount of money equivalent to rent in kind on the land they worked. In each of these cases, the lords appropriated a large part of what the serfs produced, while the serfs did their best to hold on to what they needed to survive and raise future generations.

Feudal societies were basically agricultural, and political rule within feudal societies was fragmented in comparison to that of the slave empires they replaced. Extravagant consumption by the feudal lords obstructed production. Economic production was limited to that needed for consumption with no excess for reinvestment to expand the forces of production. In time, a new class and a new mode of production appeared within the old feudal societies. We'll discuss the rise of capitalism in Chapter 3.

From what has been said so far, however, the following point should be clear: When we consider a wide variety of societies over a long period of time, a pattern of change that conforms pretty well to the little historical sketch given in the previous section becomes apparent. In the broadcast outline, this pattern runs from (1) communal societies, to (2) societies dependent on slave labor, to (3) feudal societies, and then to (4) capitalist societies, or societies dominated by the capitalist mode of production.

Of course, this should not be taken as a hard-and-fast formula without exceptions. In a letter to a Russian friend, Marx wrote that he did not intend to impose a "marching order" on history, such that each people has to pass through a neat sequence of historical stages, from slavery through feudalism and capitalism. Other Marxists have corroborated this point. The historian Walter Rodney, for example, has noted that in central and southern Africa the use of slaves did not play a central part in societies that developed out of communalism. Furthermore, Marx discussed at least one other sort of society that was dominated by what he referred to in his preface to *A Critique of Political Economy* and elsewhere as the "Asiatic mode of production." This mode of production was characteristic of civilizations as diverse as those of ancient India, Egypt, and China as well as the Aztec and Inca empires and the Ottoman empire for much of its existence. In these and other civilizations, communal villages, sometimes located throughout a far-flung river region, were united by an imperial court or a despotic leadership. A system of officials collected tribute or supervised common labor, to support the construction and maintenance of irrigation and flood-control systems, as well as an administration, an army, priests, and the imperial court.

We should not conclude that history—that is, the histories of many different societies—is an unbroken and irreversible process of using new inventions and technologies to make it possible for fewer people to produce more in less time. The founders of Marxism knew full well something that contemporary technological determinists do not seem to have realized: In the past, less productive economic practices (such as the earliest forms of feudalism in Europe) have sometimes replaced more productive practices (such as the production that took place on large estates in the latter years of the Roman Empire). Of course, it is fair to conclude from a survey of different histories of a wide range of different societies that in general the productivity of labor has risen.

Nevertheless, this is simply a factual conclusion that does not require us to believe that there is any overarching goal of history, such as better inventions or increased productivity of labor. Although some Marxists view a possible future society without exploitation as the end destination toward which history is marching, others view such a future simply as a goal that Marxists must consciously work and fight for if it is ever to be achieved.

It would also be a mistake to assume that the economic practice of a society is typically reducible to only one mode of production. This is an important point, especially in the modern period, when within many societies more than one mode of production may exist side by side. In North Africa, for example, slavery existed for a long time within the context of feudalism. And today, in some regions that used to be colonies of Europe, feudalism continues to exist in one form or another alongside capitalism.

At the same time, however, it is almost always possible from case to case to identify one mode of production as the dominant mode of production, or the mode of production that determines the character of the society more than any other. As we will see in Chapter 5, in the case of the United States, for example, monopoly capitalism is by far the most important mode of production today. It is also possible to identify an older, dying mode of production existing side by side with a new, rising mode of production. I have already mentioned this in relation to ancient Rome, and in Chapter 3, I will say a few words about how societies dominated by the feudal mode of production gave birth to *capitalism*.

Class

As we have seen, a society is a structure somewhat like a net. Unlike a net, however, the parts that make up a society—the various practices—do not all bear more or less equal weight.

There is another important way in which a society differs from our example of the net. As I have said, a society is a whole, and as a whole it is a unity of parts. Unlike many things viewed as wholes, however, a society is a whole composed of parts that are in tension with one another. This tension is especially acute in the case of societies divided along class lines, such as the capitalist societies in which we live. Let's consider this in a bit more detail, before drawing this chapter to a close.

What Is a Society?

Most of us are used to hearing that workers depend on capitalists. From one point of view, of course, this is true: Workers must work for capitalists in order to pay rent and buy food. It is also true, of course, that capitalists depend on workers, since they need to employ workers to operate their factories and offices. These are two characteristic relations of production under capitalism—or two halves of one relation. We are rarely reminded of the fact, however, that capitalists and workers form two opposing forces that often clash violently. Capitalists, for example, usually want to lengthen the workday and force down wages, whereas workers want to cut the workday and receive higher wages. Bloody battles have been fought over these issues in one capitalist society after another.

From this we can see that the tension within a capitalist society is not the sort of tension that exists within the unity of, say, a fishbowl containing two hostile fish. The unity of the fishbowl exists regardless of whether the fish fight, eat each other, or spawn. A society, by contrast, is not a container for people the way a fishbowl is a container for fish. In fact, a society is not a container at all. On the contrary, a society divided into classes is made up in part of political practice and class conflict. Furthermore, as we have seen, in order for economic production to take place in a slave society or a feudal society—that is, in order for those societies to exist at all—exploitation must take place in one form or another. We will presently see that exploitation in a different form also takes place in capitalist societies. So evidently, the unity of a class society cannot exist without conflicting classes.

Thus, if a class society can be thought of as a whole, it must be a strange sort of whole—a whole not just containing opposing forces but actually *made up of* opposing forces and relying for its existence, its development, on the conflict between these forces. In his notes "On the Question of Dialectics,"[8] Lenin called this sort of whole—a whole that is held together and develops not in spite of the fact that but because it is made up of opposed parts—a *unity of opposites*. Traditionally, Marxists have called the sort of opposition characteristic of a unity of opposites dialectical contradiction.

Most social scientists in Western universities ignore class divisions in societies and assume that the existing state of affairs is basically harmonious and stable. Of course, they are willing to admit that problems and conflicts flare up here and there within capitalist societies today. But they don't like to view the societies in which they live as unities of opposites, perhaps because this conflicts with their assumptions about the essentially harmonious and unchanging character of existing social relations. To view a society as a unity of opposites is to recognize that it is constantly changing and to understand that forces of opposition within capitalist societies might one day shatter their unity: "The integument," as Marx put it, will "burst assunder,"[9] and revolutionary upheaval will put an end to the old society.

Returning to the question of what social classes are, Lenin defined them as:

> large groups of people which differ from each other by the place they occupy in a historically determined system of social production, by their relation (in most cases fixed and formulated in law) to the means of production, by their role in the social organization of labor, and, consequently, by the dimensions and mode of acquiring the share of the social wealth of which they dispose. Classes are groups of people one of which can appropriate the labor of another owing to the different places they occupy in a definite system of social economy.[10]

This is an excellent definition. Let's look at it more closely, focusing on four ways of identifying a social group as a class: (1) the group's position within a mode of production; (2) the relationship of group members to the means of production; (3) their role in the social organization of labor, especially with reference to the ability to appropriate surplus product; and (4) the amount of social wealth group members dispose of.

1. Classes differ from one another depending on the place they occupy in a mode of production. Accordingly, in order to identify a class, one must take into account the dominant, or most important, mode of production in that society. In a society dominated by slavery, the most important classes would be slaves and slave owners, whereas in a society dominated by the capitalist mode of production, the most important classes would be the capitalists and the wage earners. Slavery existed in ancient Rome and in the United States, for almost half of its history. In the United States, however, large slave owners sold cotton and other raw materials produced by slaves to capitalist textile firms and other industries. Thus, slavery in the United States existed within the wider context of a capitalist society. This seemingly technical point has weighty political implica-

tions: By first identifying the dominant mode of production in a society, we avoid making the sort of mistake that absolves capitalists of responsibility for the existence of slavery in the United States.
2. Classes differ from one another depending on their relationship to the means of production. One or more classes within a society will have possession, legal ownership, or control of the means of production. Other classes won't. Examples of the first sort of class are slave owners, feudal lords, and capitalists. Examples of the second sort of class are slaves, tenant farmers, and wage earners.
3. A class is a social group that shares in common an ability or inability to appropriate a surplus product in a manner determined by a given mode of production. This claim is related to the second point in an obvious way: As long as one social group owns and controls the means of production, another group will have to work longer than the time necessary to maintain their own existence, in order to produce the surplus product appropriated by the first group. Economic *exploitation* occurs when one social group regularly appropriates the surplus product produced by another group. Over and over again, from one society to the next and down through the centuries, exploitation has gone hand in hand with violent class conflict.

At this point, a brief detour is necessary in order to dispel the following old story: Because workers can invest in corporate stock, every worker can become a capitalist. In exchange for their money, these investors receive a small portion or "share" of what is, legally speaking, ownership in a company. Thus, thanks to the appearance of joint stock companies, or corporations, the difference between capitalists and workers is disappearing without any revolution. Or so the story goes.

This story is not entirely inaccurate. It is true that in the United States, for instance, small shareholders, including workers, hold a significant amount of corporate stock.[11] It is also true that each small shareholder has a legal claim to ownership of some small portion of the means of production and the legal right to receive a definite portion of the company's income. In a sense, then, if workers make a profit on the stock market, they share in the exploitation of their own class. From this it would appear that a person can belong to more than one class at a time. Recognizing this, some Marxists have held that factory workers who receive 5 percent of their income from stock dividends are, so to speak, one-twentieth capitalists.

More significantly, however, small individual stockholders have little or no real voice when it comes to decisions regarding investments, hiring and firing, research and development, marketing, resource allocation, capitalization, mergers, and so on. Only the small minority of shareholders who own huge blocks of shares has a significant impact on corporate policy. Experience has shown that a big capitalist need own only one-third of the shares in a corporation to gain control of the whole undertaking. Furthermore, unlike small investors, big investors have plans, advisors, and up-to-the-minute information about the market. Thus, a handful of huge investors control not only their own investments but also the investments of many small shareholders; they do what they please with other people's money, while passing on the biggest risks to small investors. In this way, small shareholders actually help to extend the power of the biggest shareholders. This is a part of the larger picture that the familiar old story leaves out.

4. Because members of a class play a certain role in social production, they tend to be rich or poor, educated or uneducated. Clearly, capitalists will tend to have a much higher income than workers because the former exploit the latter. To illustrate this point, let us take a quick look at the distribution of total income and wealth within a capitalist society. We'll turn to the United States because well-financed propagandists would like us all to believe that there are no deep class divisions there.

By 1990 the total income of the richest 1 percent of families in the United States, after taxes, was about the same as the total income shared by the poorest 40 percent. The income of the richest 5 percent of these families in the early 1990s was about the same as that of the entire bottom 60 percent, and the richest tenth receive more money income than the poorest half.

Wealth is even more unequally distributed than income. In July of 1986 the Joint Economic Committee of the U.S. Congress reported that the richest 10 percent of families in the United States own 71.7

percent of the country's wealth, and the top one-half of 1 percent (0.5%) of U.S. families own 35.1 percent of all privately held wealth. The top 1 percent of families in the United States own 42 percent of the net wealth of all U.S. families, including 60 percent of all corporate stock and 80 percent of all family owned trusts. According to recent statistics, a mere one-fifth of 1 percent (0.2 %) of those who spend money in the United States own two-thirds of all publicly held industrial stock. One-tenth of 1 percent (0.1%) of all corporations own 60 percent of all corporate assets. The average household in the wealthiest one-half of 1 percent had about 223 times more wealth than the average household in the lower 90 percent. In other words, 1.25 million "super rich" people in the United States own more wealth than the 210 million people in the bottom 90 percent.

Taking wealth and income together, it becomes clear that the gap between rich and poor in the United States is enormous. Furthermore, according to the Joint Economic Committee, the gap between rich and poor, which remained more or less constant throughout most of the twentieth century, has gaped wider and wider from the 1970s to the 1990s. After adjusting for inflation, workers' wages have fallen in recent years. The size of the average household in the United States has decreased along with birthrates, and the number of breadwinners per household has risen as women have joined the workforce. And yet, by many measurements, the standard of living in the United States has dropped, while social services have been cut back from their dismally low level before 1973.

The gap between rich and poor in the United States strongly confirms the Marxist view that there are sharp class divisions in that supposedly classless society. We should keep in mind, however, that Marxists do not distinguish one class from another solely or even mainly by looking at differences in income and wealth. It would be more accurate to say that huge differences of income and wealth are a *result* of class divisions, rather than a defining trait of class societies.

By the way, Marxists do not view class membership as a matter of lifestyle or personal identification. A capitalist and an autoworker in the United States may both claim they are members of the middle class, but this does not mean that they are actually members of the same class. In fact, neither of them may have a very clear idea of what they mean by "middle class." An accurate understanding on the part of many people that they are members of a class is another result of political struggle. Independent working-class organizations such as militant unions and Communist parties are at once both results and contributing factors to revolutionary class consciousness.

The class structure of a society may be very complicated, and it is seldom a straightforward task to gain an accurate picture of class structure. In some so-called "underdeveloped countries" of Africa, for example, the capitalist middlemen who connect native labor with foreign capital may be communal chieftains or rely on feudal relations of allegiance; the peasantry in such a country may be under feudal domination and yet play an important role in providing cheap food for urban workers; and other people—including shopkeepers, small farmers, self-employed truck and taxi drivers, low-level managers, administrators, and bureaucrats—may form one or more different kinds of middle class. It takes close study, then, to identify the various classes that coexist in such a society.

Furthermore, in order to gain a more detailed picture of the class structure of a society, it is useful to distinguish different groups, or *strata* within the various classes, on the basis of secondary considerations such as income, ideological allegiance, political function, profession, and so on. Thus, in many societies today there is an important strata of intellectuals. These may be teachers, students, bureaucrats, technicians, priests, or some other social group, depending on the society.

Summary

Key terms discussed in this chapter include *society* (or *social formation*), *social practices, structure, unity of opposites, use-value, goods, labor, means of production, economic base* and *superstructure, productive forces, relations of production, mode of production, commodity production, exploitation,* and *class.*

It should be clear from this discussion so far that Marxists view a society not as a gathering of ready-made people and institutions but as a complex whole made up of certain social processes, or practices. One of these practices that can be found in every society is the production of goods, or economic practice.

Forces and relations of production are important aspects of economic practice. Certain forces of production in combination with certain relations of production make up a mode of production.

Slavery, feudalism, and the capitalist mode of production are each characterized by specific forms of exploitation. Large social groups differ from other such groups within a society, in part according to whether the members of these groups exploit or are exploited and the manner in which they exploit or are exploited. These large groups are the various social classes.

Much more remains to be said. From what has been said in this chapter alone, however, it should already be clear that historical materialists have their hands full when it comes to making what Lenin called "a concrete analysis of a concrete situation." Far from being a rigid dogma, historical materialism is a coherent but open theory of social change that provides us with the concepts and methodology for explaining complex social and historical realities that "mainstream social scientists" overlook.

Reading List

*Engels, Friedrich, and Karl Marx. *The Communist Manifesto* (also published under the title *The Manifesto of the Communist League*). The *Manifesto* was written in 1847 and published in February 1848 at the request of a group Marx helped found called the Communist League.

As Marx's biographer Franz Mehring pointed out, in the *Manifesto* Marx and Engels wrote about some developments as though they had already happened, including large-scale machine production, the concentration of capital, the development of a global capitalist market, expansion of the means of communication, changes in working-class family relations, and widespread public education. All of these developments took place in Germany just as Marx and Engels predicted, of course; nevertheless, they did not take place until years or even decades after the *Manifesto* was written.

In their later years, Marx and Engels continued to uphold the *Manifesto*, although some of their ideas had changed. For example, in a letter dated April 9, 1870, Marx noted that the working class in England had become divided into Irish and English workers. In this letter he seems to have abandoned the view expressed in the *Manifesto* that, thanks to capitalism, "national differences and antagonisms between peoples are vanishing more and more each day."[12] Furthermore, after the lessons of the Paris Commune of 1871, Marx and Engels also abandoned their view that it was possible for workers to gain political power without destroying a large part of the capitalist state.

Other Marxists have also corrected some of the ideas in the *Manifesto*. Lenin, for example, recognized that some workers in the richest capitalist countries benefit at least a little from their countries' domination of poorer countries in Asia, Africa, and Latin America. Because of this, many workers in the richest countries certainly believe they have more to lose than just their chains. We'll return to this subject in Chapter 5.

———. *The German Ideology* (abridged edition). New York: International Publishers, 1970. A broad philosophical outline in which Marx and Engels "settled accounts" with some of the idealist notions they believed as youths.

Lenin, V.I. *The Teachings of Karl Marx*. New York: International Publishers, 1930. Some of the views on Marxist philosophy in Lenin's essay of roughly thirty pages differ slightly from the views presented in this current primer. Still, Lenin's book is a good introduction for a systematic study of historical materialism.

*Marx, Karl. "1857 Introduction" to the *Grundrisse: Introduction to the Critique of Political Economy*. New York: Vintage, 1973. The *Grundrisse* was a rough draft for *Capital* and was not intended to be published. The "Introduction" appears on pp. 81–111 in the inexpensive Vintage edition. Despite the rough writing style and a difficult manner of expression borrowed from the German philosopher G.W.F. Hegel, the thirty or so pages of the "Introduction" provide one of the best short explanations by Marx himself of his differences with previous political economists, his views on the sciences, and his study of modes of production that predate capitalism.

———. Preface to *A Contribution to a Critique of Political Economy*. (Also published under the title: A *Critique of Political Economy*.) Published in numerous collections. The preface, written in 1859, is little more than four or five pages long. It begins with Marx's short account of how his scientific ideas developed, and it also contains a thumbnail sketch of Marx's materialist conception of history. For better or for worse, these few pages have become one of the most influential presentations of historical materialism.

———. *Pre-Capitalist Economic Formations*. New York: International Publishers, 1965.

Vladimir Ilyich Lenin (1870–1924)

Founders of Historical Materialism

The real question that arises in appraising the social activity of an individual is: What conditions ensure the success of his actions, what guarantee is there that these actions will not remain an isolated act lost in a welter of contrary acts?

—*V.I. Lenin*

Part of V.I. Lenin's answer to this question with regard to the social activity of workers was that the most committed of them should join *vanguard parties*, or militant and tightly organized parties capable of leading masses during periods of revolutionary upsurge. On this point he disagreed with his comrade Rosa Luxemburg, who held that revolutionary parties—at least in countries with long traditions of representative democracy—should come closer to encompassing the whole organized working class, if they are to win state power and remain truly revolutionary.

As both Lenin and Luxemburg saw it, the internal organization of a fighting Marxist party must be based on the principles of *democratic centralism*. These principles are: collective leadership and division of labor under the direction of a central body consisting of elected representatives; election of representatives from lower to higher bodies by majority vote; accountability of all representatives, including the right to recall them at a moment's notice; conscious and voluntary acceptance of party decisions by every party member; subordination of the decisions of lower bodies to those of higher bodies, with practical decisions binding on all party members; and open debate and criticism.

It is important to keep in mind that democratic centralism is not a set of principles for organizing a state or a society. Rather, it is a set of principles for organizing militant workers' parties. There is a big difference between a voluntary political organization and a state, between a party program and a state constitution, and between party rules, which are binding on members who have freely decided to accept party discipline, and the laws of a state, which apply across the board to everyone within the borders of the state. If the principles of democratic centralism are forced onto people willy-nilly, then, as Luxemburg warned, the result will be the sort of *bureaucratic* centralism that came to characterize the regimes of eastern Europe.

* * *

A book by Lenin's wife, Nadezhda Krupskaya, *Reminiscences of Lenin*, is a revealing portrait of her husband, the revolutionary and the man. Unfortunately, however, at the time she wrote the book she had been isolated by Stalin, and the book was subjected to censorship. Thus, Krupskaya's biography contains unfair attacks against Stalin's enemies, some of whom, including Leon Trotsky and Nikolai Bukharin, were among Lenin's closest comrades.

Notes

1. Karl Marx, *Capital* Vol. 1 (New York: International Publishers, 1967), p. 35.

2. The most important exception to the rule is land that has not been fenced in, drained, cleared, fertilized, or "improved" in some other way. Nevertheless, as Marx showed in the third volume of *Capital,* the value of "unimproved" land depends indirectly on the value of commodities that are products of labor.

3. Karl Marx, *Capital* Vol. 1, p. 43.

4. David McLellan, ed., *Karl Marx: Selected Writings* (Oxford: Oxford University Press, 1977), p. 389.

5. Of course, not all relations and human actions involve production. It doesn't appear to be particularly useful to view selling, for example, as production.

6. McLellan, ed., *Karl Marx,* p. 157.

7. For over a thousand years, at any rate, until early capitalism made the reintroduction of slavery profitable in North America and elsewhere.

8. Refer to the reading list for chapter 1.

9. McLellan, ed., *Karl Marx,* p. 487.

10. V.I. Lenin, *Collected Works* Vol. 29 (Moscow: Progress Publishers, 1965), p. 421.

11. By the way, the fact that many workers in the richest capitalist countries have had money to invest in stocks is related to developments I will discuss in Chapter 5.

12. Marx's letter to Siegfried Meyer and August Vogt appears in McLellan, ed., *Karl Marx,* pp. 591–592.

3

The Capitalist Mode of Production

The Yankee industrialist Andrew Carnegie once claimed that God gave him his money. As silly as this claim sounds, some mainstream economists spend a lot of time putting much the same message more subtly. They expect us to believe that capitalists earn—and thus deserve—their wealth because they work hard, save their money instead of squandering it, look to the future, take risks, keep their eyes open for new opportunities to produce things that people want, or perform some other daring, useful, or virtuous task. There may be some small bit of truth in all of this; nevertheless, this sort of account is not much better than Andrew Carnegie's story. Marx offered an alternative account.

As we saw in Chapter 2, economic production in a capitalist society is typically production for the market, or commodity production. We will examine commodity production in more detail in the following section. A capitalist society, however, is not just any society in which there is commodity production. Later in this chapter we will consider how capitalism differs from simple commodity production.

Commodity Production

As we saw in Chapter 2, all commodities satisfy human wants. In other words, all commodities are use-values. To view a commodity as a use-value is to focus on its qualities and properties, its shape, size, color, smell, and so on. Thus, to take our example of bread, this commodity may be a use-value because it is edible, contains lots of vitamins, or tastes and smells good.

Because commodities are produced for exchange, however, they must embody some sort of value in addition to use-value. After all, traders and merchants are interested in commodities not because commodities have certain qualities that satisfy some want or need when they are consumed but rather because they are of value in exchange. Commodities are also *exchange-values*, then, irrespective of their particular qualities or the wants and needs they satisfy.

Exchange-value (or what Marxists sometimes simply call *value*) appears first as a ratio in which a certain number or measure of useful things of one kind is exchanged for a certain number or measure of useful things of another kind. Millions of such exchanges take place every day, equating very different use-values with one another. A small lump of twenty-four karat gold, for example, might exchange for four loaves of bread or one cotton shirt.

All lumps of twenty-four karat gold can be compared regardless of their shapes or sizes. This is because all twenty-four karat gold has something in common that makes comparison possible: weight. This is true of all commodities: In order for them to be compared in exchange, commodities must have something in common that can be measured. But what is it?

Bread and cotton shirts are commodities produced from different raw materials by different laborers with very different tools and skills, and they satisfy very different wants. So again the question arises: What do all the articles in this wide array of things that are constantly exchanged one for another have in common? As we know, bread, shirts, gold, and all other commodities (with the exception of the special case of "unimproved" land) are products of labor. The sort of work it takes to produce four loaves of bread, however, is very different from the sort of work it takes to produce a cotton shirt. A baker mixes and kneads dough, stokes ovens, and engages in other specific activities, crafts, or forms of concrete labor, whereas a shirtmaker engages in entirely different forms of concrete labor.

At the same time workers are involved in concrete labor, they also form part of a social labor force that collectively supplies a society with its necessities, conveniences, and luxuries. A baker can be viewed as someone who makes bread. But a baker can also be viewed as having something in common with an autoworker, a computer programmer, and every other member of society who produces goods. To do this we must view the baker's labor not as this or that *sort* of labor but simply as one small part of the total expenditure of human energy in the course of economic production in a society as a whole. Similarly, the autoworker, the computer programmer, and all other workers can be viewed as taking part in uniform, general, or *abstract labor*. Abstract labor, then, is labor in general, viewed without regard to its particular characteristics or purposes. Despite their varied appearances, the commodities that surround us are all the result of abstract labor.

But why go to the trouble of drawing a distinction between abstract and concrete labor? Because only by distinguishing between abstract and concrete labor can we grasp how a wide variety of commodities can be compared and exchanged the way they in fact are. Abstract labor is what all productive labor—that is, all labor that results in the creation of goods and services—has in common. Furthermore, abstract labor, like exchange-value, can be determined by measurement, rather than by identifying purposes and properties, as in the case of concrete labor, or by identifying qualities and subjective wants, as in the case of use-value. Just as all pieces of twenty-four karat gold can be measured by weight and exchanged on that basis, and just as an exchange-value can be measured as a number or amount of other commodities, abstract labor can be measured in terms of labor time. In creating exchange-value, then, it is not the concrete labor that counts but the fact that labor *in general,* abstract labor, is expended in doing this work.

Of course, just as twenty-four karat gold differs in purity from eighteen-karat gold, so also labor varies in the degree of skill and training it involves. As we know, products of more skilled labor, such as watches, are exchanged (and thus equated) with products of less skilled labor, such as fruit. In this way, labor of different levels of skill is compared.

But how is this comparison carried out? According to Marx, unskilled labor counts as a sort of baseline against which labor of all degrees of skill and training is compared: "Skilled labor counts only as simple labor intensified, or rather, as multiplied simple labor, a given amount of skilled labor being equated with a greater amount of unskilled, or simple labor."[1] Just as three ounces of twenty-four karat gold equals four ounces of eighteen-karat gold, one hour of one sort of skilled labor may be equal to five hours of unskilled labor. As with so many other social processes, of course, few people involved in exchange are actually aware of comparing labor of different degrees of skill. As Marx noted, "The different proportions in which different sorts of labor are reduced to unskilled labor as their standard are established by a social process that goes on behind the backs of the producers, and consequently appears to be fixed by custom."[2]

To sum up, the fact that all commodities are products of labor means that they embody some specific part of the total labor that has gone into the production of masses of commodities entering into exchange. They are equal or unequal insofar as they represent equal or unequal parts of the total product of a society—insofar, that is, as they embody a smaller or larger share of the sum total of labor time expended in production. Thus, exchange-value is determined by abstract labor.

But if the value of a commodity depends on the labor time spent in producing it, then shouldn't commodities produced by lazier and less efficient workers be more valuable because they take longer to produce? Evidently this is not the case. A less skillful artisan may ask a higher price for his commodities, but if buyers can purchase the commodity at a lower price from someone else, they probably will. In commodity exchange, what counts is not the time that an individual producer may have taken to make a particular commodity but the time it normally takes, or the average time it takes many producers competing with each other to produce the same sort of commodity.

Clearly, the average time it takes to produce a cotton shirt will be much lower in a society in which power looms are widely used than in a society with only hand looms. As more efficient methods of production are introduced and become widespread, the *average socially necessary labor time* for the production of each commodity falls, and as a result, its exchange-value also falls. Thus, the measure or magnitude of the exchange-value of any good is the amount of labor time required for the production of the commodity within a given society, with a given level of development of the forces of production, including technology. As such, each commodity represents only a certain part of socially necessary labor time. To put it briefly, then, we can say that the magnitude of value is determined by the amount of *average, socially necessary labor time* "wrapped up" in a use-value. This is a statement of what Marxists call the *law of value*.

Of course, it is not true that in all exchanges the labor time embodied in commodities exchanged has always been equivalent. When bread is in short supply, for example, one cotton shirt may exchange for three loaves instead of the usual one shirt for four loaves. Conversely, if there is a glut of bread or a shortage of shirts on the market, one shirt may exchange for five loaves of bread. Supply and demand, then, accounts in part for deviations from the law of value. As a result of competition, however, and as more goods enter into exchange, commodities *tend* to exchange at their value over a period of time. (As it turns out, in fully developed capitalist societies commodities tend to exchange at what economists call their prices of production. The relationship between value and prices of production is a complicated issue and a topic of much debate among Marxists today. Marx, however, believed that the tendency of commodities to exchange at their prices of production depends on the principle that labor time determines value.)

Eventually, commodities come to be valued in terms of one handy commodity that is readily taken in exchange by buyers and sellers. Salt remained one such commodity in some parts of eastern Africa well into the twentieth century. One could take a certain measure of salt in exchange for, say, a head of cattle, secure in the knowledge that one could later exchange a measure of the salt for a measure of vegetables, another measure for a certain amount of rice, and so on. Thus, in many societies, one universally exchangeable commodity came to be used as a "go-between" in sales and purchases and as a commonly accepted measure of value of all commodities. This commodity, whether it takes the form of salt, cowry shells, gold, paper, or something else, is *money*.[3]

Roughly speaking, the exchange-value of a commodity expressed in money tends to be its *price*. In modern capitalism prices generally tend to rise above value in boom times and fall below during economic slumps. Nevertheless, according to Marx, exchange-value is the center of gravity around which actual market prices fluctuate according to supply and demand, among other factors (including price-setting by monopolies, tax policies, state subsidies, and other considerations).

So far we have taken a very brief look at commodity production in general. In order to understand modern capitalism better, we need to examine what makes the capitalist mode of production different from simple commodity production. This we will do in the following section.

Capitalist Exploitation

In *Capital*, Marx described how a new class was formed gradually in Europe in the later Middle Ages, as large landowners pushed peasants off land in the countryside and into the cities, and as poor artisans in the cities came to be employed by rich artisans. The rich artisans who owned means of production—workshops, tools, raw materials, and so on—hired workers. These workers, who did not own the means of production they worked up and operated, were early wage laborers. Marxists have sometimes referred to wage laborers simply as workers.

At first the wealthy artisans might have worked alongside their employees, but with the passage of time and the hiring of more workers, the output of the wealthy artisans' workshops came to be almost entirely dependent on the labor of the workers. Because so many of the first employers of wage laborers lived in cities and were opposed to feudal rulers in the countryside, they came to be known as the bourgeoisie, which is the French word for "townspeople." Marxists have sometimes called societies dominated by the capitalist mode of production bourgeois societies.

In the capitalist mode of production, the only thing wage laborers have to sell from day to day is their ability to work—their strength, skill, and technical knowledge. Marxists call the strength, skill, and technical knowledge of workers *labor-power*. It is important to notice that the ability to work is different from the use of this ability, just as a tractor is different from the use to which that tractor can be put, or a loaf of bread is different from its consumption. As the wage earner works for the capitalist, the capitalist uses, or consumes, a certain amount of the labor-power he has just purchased from the worker. And in the course of consuming this labor-power, the capitalist receives its use-value, labor.

In a society of simple commodity producers, labor-power is not for sale: Butchers, bakers, and candlestick makers own their own tools, which they themselves use to produce commodities. In a capitalist society, by contrast, those who own factories, raw materials, instruments of production, and other means of production can and do buy labor-power whenever they hire workers. *Wages* represent the price of labor-power. The two chief forms of wages are time wages (hourly wages and salaries) and piece wages (so much paid per item of output). If, for example, an experienced worker earning a minimum of six dollars an hour on average assembles three widgets an hour, the capitalist could set piece wages at two dollars for each widget assembled. In this sense, then, piece wages are nothing but a changed form of time wages.

Despite what public relations firms would like us to believe—and even despite how an individual capitalist might honestly describe his motivations—capitalists as a class do not hire workers primarily in order to provide the workers with an income, make workers feel useful, or to produce useful things. Capitalists hire workers because by doing so they, the capitalists, stand to make a profit. Those who for whatever reason keep unproductive workers on the payroll find themselves at a disadvantage relative to the competition. As soon as it is no longer profitable to keep workers on the payroll, capitalists fire them by the hundreds and thousands. In other words, as most of us suspect, capitalists typically conduct their affairs in conformity with the profit motive.

But how do capitalists make a profit by hiring workers? To answer this question, we need to take a look at commodity production under capitalism. For the sake of illustration, let's take a trip to a carpentry shop and "break down" the cost of producing a chair with a wholesale value of sixty dollars. To make things simpler, we'll ignore the very difficult problem of the relationship between price and value and simply assume for the sake of illustration that costs of production directly reflect the value of commodities.

Part of the value of the finished chair is the value of the wood, glue, shellac, and other raw materials used up in the production of the chair. This value is passed down the production line and is embodied unchanged in the finished chair. Let's say the total value of this item is ten dollars.

A second part of the value of the chair is the value of the part of the carpentry shop, saws, sanders, electricity, and so on that get used up in the production process. When the owner of the shop calculates costs of production, he includes an item of "overhead" and "depreciation," based on the average life of the instruments of production used up, to cover wear and tear on premises, tools, and machinery and replacement of worn-out parts. This calculation is a recognition by the capitalist that a portion of the value of the shop building, machinery, and so on is also passed down the production line and is embodied in the finished chair. Let's say this item of overhead and depreciation amounts to another ten dollars.

The third part of the value of the finished product represents new value added by the labor of the carpenters. Let's say it took two carpenters of equal skill working together for two hours to produce the chair. So assuming they both receive a wage of five dollars an hour, the owner of the carpentry shop has laid out a total of twenty dollars in wages to produce the chair. This new value added is also embodied in the finished chair.

Taking all of this into account, the cost of producing the chair breaks down as follows:

Raw materials	$10
Overhead and depreciation	10
Labor-power (wages)	20
Total cost of production	$40

Notice, however, that the exchange-value of the finished chair is sixty dollars. (This, of course, was just a figure we came up with for the sake of illustration. Nevertheless, the exchange-value of the chair would have to be considerably greater than its total cost of production, in order to make it profitable for the capitalist to engage in producing chairs in the first place. The capitalist, remember, conducts business in conformity with the profit motive: If it is unprofitable to produce chairs, a capitalist will cease to do so.) In Marx's terminology, the twenty-dollar difference between the cost of production and the exchange-value of the chair is *surplus value*.

Profit is that part of surplus value that goes into the pocket of an individual capitalist. Thus, in our example, the profit going to the owner of the carpenter's shop would be that part of the twenty dollars that remains after the owner has paid landlords, lawyers, and tax collectors and set aside money for future production.

But what is the source of surplus value? In other words, in our example, where does the twenty-dollar difference between cost of production and value come from?

As we have seen, the values that the capitalist acquires in the form of means of production (raw materials as well as factory buildings, machines, and so on) pass unchanged into the value of the finished product. Since labor-power is the only remaining cost of production we identified in our breakdown, surplus value must be the result of using this commodity. The source of surplus value, then, must be labor.

This conclusion is consistent with the observation that workers sell their *labor-power* to the capitalist for wages, not their contributions to production: Having bought a certain quantity of labor-power, individual capitalists may put it to work wastefully or efficiently, just as they may use the gasoline they have purchased to fuel more or less energy-efficient engines. The more efficiently workers work, the greater the value added during the production process. Labor-power, then, must be a commodity that, when it is used, has the peculiar property of creating value greater than its own value. In order to understand how this can be so, we need to find out how to determine the value of this peculiar commodity, labor-power.

As we have seen, the value of commodities typically depends on the average socially necessary labor time required for their production. The same is true of labor-power as a commodity: The value of labor-power depends upon the amount of labor time that must be expended to produce it. But how is labor-power produced? Certainly not in a shop, factory, or office!

Labor-power exists only in living human beings. In order for humans to live, they must have means of subsistence, and in order for labor-power to continue to exist, workers must reproduce themselves—they must raise children. Therefore, one consideration for calculating the value of labor-power is that workers must have sufficient means of subsistence not only for themselves but also for their children, to guarantee the suppy of labor-power for the next generation.

The value of labor-power also varies according to the kind of work done. More special instruction and materials are needed to reproduce a computer programmer's labor-power than to reproduce a janitor's. Thus, another consideration for calculating the value of labor-power is the amount of labor time expended for education, training, and instruction of workers.

Furthermore, the number and character of a worker's wants as well as the ways of satisfying them vary from one society to another, from one historical period to another, and from one climatic setting to another. Marx noted that English workers need beer, whereas French workers need wine. Moreover, a Siberian worker, unlike a Sri Lankan worker, needs a heavy coat. This is why Marx insisted that the determination of the value of labor-power depends on average socially prescribed needs.

The value of labor-power, then, resolves itself into a definite quantity of commodities and services that meet the worker's "customary and historically developed needs"; commodities required for the maintenance of a household, both of the worker and the worker's family; and expenses of education and training. To state it as briefly as possible, then, the value of labor-power is the average socially necessary labor time required to reproduce it. Accordingly, if we were to calculate the value of all the commodities and services involved in producing labor-power in a certain society at a certain period of time, we would have calculated the value of that labor-power.

Now, let us say that the workers in the carpentry shop work eight hours a day producing chairs. Let us further say that to provide the average socially prescribed food, clothing, shelter, and so on that workers need to recuperate their labor-power, they need a basket of articles and services, the total value of which is equal to forty dollars. In our example, each hour of work results in ten dollars of added value (that is, five dollars represented by wages plus five dollars of surplus value). So in the course of the last four hours of an eight-hour workday the workers produce new value, the money value of which is forty dollars each, for which the capitalist does not pay them. From this, we can see that even though the owner of the shop has paid full value for the labor-power added to the product (that is, forty dollars in wages), that labor-power has cost the capitalist the value of only four of the eight hours of labor time added to the product. In our example, then, half of the workday is paid and the other half is unpaid.

Surplus value, then, turns out to be the value workers produce over and above the value of their labor-power. In Marx's terminology, the ratio of surplus value to wages is the *rate of surplus value,* or the *rate of exploitation.* Thus the rate of exploitation of the workers in our carpentry shop is 40:40, or 100 percent.

* * *

Before proceeding to the next section, this might be a good place to say a few words about a term that often turns up in discussions of Marxism: *alienation.* In his *Economic and Philosophic Manuscripts of 1844,*[4] Marx noted that, with the advent of capitalism, the more productive workers are, the less control they seem to have over their conditions of life. Increasingly, workers have come to view the products of their own hands and brains as having existed before they were produced and having emerged from an alien and hostile source to dominate them. Furthermore, with the decline of earlier traditional bonds that submerged each individual within a larger community, workers and capitalists alike—finding themselves surrounded by such products of "alienated labor"—came to feel increasingly separated from their own life activity. The young Marx referred to this sense of separation or fragmentation as self-alienation.

Although the word *alienation* continues to appear from time to time in Marx's later works,[5] he began as early as 1845 to move away from the views he expressed in the *Economic and Philosophic Manuscripts.* The work remained unpublished until 1932. Interest in alienation was rekindled almost ten years before that, however, with the appearance in 1923 of Georg Lukacs's book *History and Class Consciousness*.[6]

Alienation remains a controversial topic today, and Marxists disagree among themselves about the meaning of the word. Indeed, some Marxists believe that the notion is so vague or speculative that it is more trouble than it is worth. Still, discussions of alienation strike a responsive chord for many people who sense a loss of community, derive little satisfaction from their jobs, and feel that in some sense their own lives and personalities have lost cohesiveness.

Capital

Returning to the main line of the presentation, let us raise our sights above the carpentry shop, to take in a view of society as a whole.

Capitalists as a class pay millions of workers' wages, which enable workers continuously to reproduce their labor-power at the service of capitalists. By their labor, as we have seen, workers not only pay their own wages but also create surplus value, which is the source of the capitalists' income. (Surplus value flows into the pockets of the capitalist class by a hundred different channels: Part goes to landowners for rent, part goes to the state in the form of taxes, and so on.)

Capitalists, however, do not use all of their surplus value to satisfy their personal needs, wants, and whims. Rather, they apply part of it to additional production by extending their enterprises, hiring more workers, upgrading their machinery, and so on. A larger workforce in turn produces for the capitalist a greater quantity of surplus value, and in this way capitalist enterprises grow larger. Capitalists who do not regularly plow back a portion of surplus value into expanded production find themselves unable to compete with other capitalists. It is important to notice that this is not true of simple commodity producers: A baker who exchanges four loaves of bread for a cotton shirt, which he then puts on his back, has no surplus to plow back into expanded production of more bread.

The portion of surplus value that capitalists regularly plow back into production is *capital*. Capital may take any of a number of forms: It may be in the form of money, machinery, raw materials, land, factory buildings, or finished commodities. Whatever form capital takes, however, its value is of such a kind as serves for the production of new value.

We will recall from our example of the production of the chair that the value of the capital expended for the means of production (raw materials, machinery, tools, and the like) is transferred unchanged (all at once or part by part) to the finished product. We also saw that the capital expended for labor-power is not transferred unchanged to the finished product, but grows in the labor process, creating surplus value. We can distinguish, then, between two parts of the total capital invested in production: (1) *constant capital,* or capital expended for the means of production, and (2) *variable capital,* or capital expended for labor-power.

As total capital grows, or *accumulates,* so does its variable section. As a factory expands and new machinery is purchased, more workers may be hired. If a certain quantity of the means of production always were to require the same quantity of labor-power to set it into motion, then obviously the demand for labor-power would grow in proportion to the growth of capital; the greater capital would grow, the greater the demand for labor-power would be. Over a period of time, however, the rate of growth of variable capital does not keep pace with the rate of growth of constant capital. This is because individual capitalists in various branches of industry apply new technologies, machines, and methods of management that enable fewer workers to produce more. Individual capitalists correctly calculate that over a period of time they will save enough in wages to make it more than worthwhile to invest in the new technologies, machines, and methods of management. By saving in wages, they will be able to sell at a lower price than their competitors and make a larger profit.

Viewed more broadly, however, the application of new technologies and methods of management and the resulting growth in the productivity of labor cause the mass of the means of production to increase more quickly than the mass of labor-power embodied in them. The demand for labor-power does not rise proportionately with the accumulation of capital, but sinks relatively. The result is what is somewhat misleadingly called the increasing capital intensive character of production, or what Marxists call the increased organic composition of capital. In this way, the same competition that drives individual capitalists to raise the productivity of labor tends to drive down the rate of profit for capitalists throughout a line of industry.

As the capital formed in the process of accumulation is requiring fewer and fewer workers relative to its size, the older, more labor-intensive capitalist enterprises are being driven out of business in the process of centralization, throwing their employees out of work. In this way there develops a large surplus mass of workers, an *industrial reserve army* made up of workers who are employed only irregularly or who are dependent on public assistance.

In the nineteenth century the most industrialized capitalist societies were shaken by periodic economic crises. Overproduction was at the source of each crisis—that is, there were not enough buyers for the goods already produced. The so-called law of supply and demand dictates that production must be stepped up to meet buyer demand for goods until a point is reached when the market is saturated with commodities. By this point, however, a large quantity of such commodities has already been produced in the factories and are on their way to the market for sale.

Meanwhile, something strange had taken place. At the same time as there was overproduction of, say, bread or cotton cloth, there were plenty of people, including bakers and textile workers themselves, who went hungry and wore rags. These people simply could not afford to buy the bread or clothes they needed to stay nourished or warm. This is an important point to keep in mind when one hears about the magical powers of "the Market" and its famous law of supply and demand. The word *demand* in this law means *effective demand*—the presence of buyers who are ready *and able* to pay a profitable price for goods—not just the presence of people who want or need those goods.

When overproduction takes place and the market is glutted, the effect on an economy is devastating. Factories shut down, large numbers of workers lose their jobs, raw materials rot in warehouses, and so on. This situation is known as *recession*. The circumstances continue until the recession reaches rock bottom and millions more workers lose their jobs and their ability to purchase new goods. Once capitalists finally unload their surplus commodities at give-away prices or their inventories have rotted away in warehouses, the demand for commodities picks up again and a new boom is under way. Capitalists hire workers, purchase new raw materials, and so on. This journey from boom to recession and back again is known as the business cycle.

Assuming that this account of things is accurate, it raises a number of questions, including the following: How can capitalists in a "capital-intensive" field such as automated steel production enjoy the same rate of profit as their fellow capitalists in a more labor-intensive industry who need to invest far less of their capital in machines, premises, raw materials, and the like and can therefore use proportionately larger quantities of living labor-power? Marx solved this problem in the third volume of *Capital* by showing that with the sale of one sort of commodity above its value and other sorts of commodities below their value the differences in profit are leveled out and an average rate of profit develops for all branches of production. Quite unconsciously and without agreement among themselves, capitalists exchange their commodities in such a fashion that all capitalists contribute the surplus value that they have extracted from their workers to a general pool, and the total result of their combined exploitation is then divided among the capitalists, and they all receive a share in accordance with the size of their own capital.

So far we have seen that the capitalists' profit comes from surplus value and that the greater the surplus value relative to wages, the greater the rate of exploitation of workers. Thus, if we oversimplify a bit, we could conclude that the struggle between capitalists and workers comes close to being a "zero-sum game": When capitalists receive greater profit, workers receive lower wages. In Chapter 5 we will see that the relationship between capitalists and some workers in the wealthiest capitalist countries is not exactly a zero-sum game, after all. Nevertheless, this observation does not change the fact that the struggle over the division of the working day and the capitalists' striving to increase surplus value are the economic basis of the class struggle. Capitalists as a class fight hard—and often violently—to increase their share of the values created by labor and to decrease the share going to the worker as wages. This they do by extending the working day without increasing wages; reducing wages without reducing the working day; and increasing output either by forcing the worker to work harder per hour for the same wage (this is called speedup), or by improving methods of production by introducing labor-saving machinery.

In addition, a large number of unemployed or underemployed workers desperately competing for a fixed number of jobs ensures that the supply of labor-power exceeds demand, forcing wages down below the value of labor-power. It is easy to see, then, that the existence of an industrial reserve army of the unemployed serves to depress the wages of employed workers and to obstruct efforts by workers to reduce the length of the working day and to oppose speedup and the introduction of labor-saving machinery.

Conversely, organized activities on the part of workers may raise the price of labor at a given site, or in a given industry. The right of workers to strike, the eight-hour workday, child labor and minimum wage laws, improved working conditions, antitrust legislation, and social security are all achievements of organized labor that have been wrenched from capitalists after long, hard, and sometimes bloody battles.

In the last quarter of the twentieth century, however, gains won by workers through generations of struggle have been eroded in the United States and other advanced capitalist countries. Unions have lost more and more power, as the length of the workday has increased and real wages have fallen. And yet, even as the capitalist class has won many battles in the class struggle, capitalism has proved incapable of solving fundamental problems such as its inability to fully use the productive capacity it has developed, the persistence of large-scale unemployment, and periodic economic crises. Indeed, as we will see in Chapter 5, more highly developed capitalism has brought with it even more catastrophic problems.

The class struggle is never waged on a level playing field. Rather, as we saw in Chapter 2 with reference to slave society, the class that gains economic dominance by appropriating the surplus product tends to subordinate much of society to its aims and attitudes. In Chapter 4 we will take a look at the political institutions used by the capitalist class to come out on top in the class struggle.

Summary

Key terms discussed in this chapter include *exchange-value* (or simply *value*), *abstract labor, average socially necessary labor time, law of value, money, price, wage, labor-power, profit, surplus value, rate of exploitation, alienation, capital, constant capital, variable capital, accumulation of capital, effective demand, industrial reserve army,* and *class struggle.*

We have mentioned three important characteristics of the capitalist mode of production: (1) commodity production; (2) ownership of means of production by part of society, but not all of it; and (3) the existence of wage laborers, who sell their ability to work, their labor-power, to capitalists.

Within such a system, labor-power has been transformed into a commodity. The value of labor-power, like the value of every other commodity, is determined by the average socially necessary labor time required to produce it—that is to say, the average cost of maintaining, educating, and training the workers and their family at a certain customary and socially determined standard of living. Capitalists, the private owners of means of production, tend to buy labor-power at or near its value. Wages are the price capitalists pay for labor-power. Having bought labor-power, a capitalist sets it to work for a day.

During the course of the workday, however, workers produce far greater value than the value of their labor-power. Workers are paid less in wages than the value their labor adds to the product. Surplus value—the value workers add to a commodity for which they are not paid—is the source of the capitalists' profit, and capitalist exploitation is the process of extracting this surplus value. Capital is the portion of surplus value that is regularly plowed back into the production of new value. The class struggle in capitalist societies is based largely on the workers' demands for higher wages and a shorter workday on the one hand, and the capitalists' struggle to maximize surplus value on the other. (Workers and capitalists also fight over control of the process of production and the speed of work, safety and work conditions, and the way in which work is organized.)

As one would expect given the complexity of economic practices today, there is much more to take into account than I have had space for in this chapter. Moreover, difficult questions remain to be answered, and many new problems are bound to appear as historical materialists grapple with theoretical problems they have already identified. Far from being an embarrassment to Marxists, however, these observations underscore a point mentioned in Chapter 1: Although historical materialism can be viewed as a coherent theory of social change, like other scientific fields, it is also wide open to future development and enrichment.

Reading List

Engels, Frederick. *Anti-Duhring*. New York: International Publishers, 1966.
    Part II of this book (pp. 161–278) is a clear summary of the first volume of *Capital*.

The Capitalist Mode of Production

Lukacs, Georg. *History and Class Consciousness: Studies in Marxist Dialectics.* Cambridge, Mass.: The MIT Press, 1971. Focusing on the theme of alienation, the brilliant Hungarian philosopher presents a very different view of Marxism from the one presented in this primer.

*Marx, Karl. *Wage Labor and Capital.* Originally a lecture Marx delivered to a working-class audience in 1847, this short essay has appeared in numerous editions and anthologies.

⎯⎯⎯. *Value, Price and Profit.* First published in 1865, this essay originally took the form of another series of lectures to a working-class audience. This text, together with the *Communist Manifesto* and *Wage Labor and Capital,* constitute a good sequence of readings for beginning students of Marxism.

*⎯⎯⎯. *Capital: A Critique of Political Economy,* Vol I. New York: International Publishers, 1967. This book is required reading for anyone who needs to understand social change and contemporary society. The first volume of *Capital* was conceived as part of a larger work, which includes the three volumes of *Capital,* together with Marx's essay *Theories of Surplus Value.* These books represent a great scientific breakthrough and a powerful theoretical weapon for enemies of capitalism.

Rosa Luxemburg (1871–1919)

Founders of Historical Materialism

Franz Mehring described Rosa Luxemburg and her comrade Clara Zetkin, the leader of the German Social Democratic Party's women's organization, as "the only real men in the social democratic movement."[7] Evidently, he meant this as a compliment. Perhaps Lenin paid Luxemburg a better compliment when he described her as an "eagle" of the revolution.[8] Like so many people today, Lenin and Mehring greatly admired Luxemburg's intelligence, strength, and ferocious courage.

Perhaps more than any other Marxist, Luxemburg has come to be associated with Marx's statement of 1879 that "The emancipation of the working class must be achieved by the working class itself."[9] According to Luxemburg, the "active, untrammeled, energetic political life of the broadest masses of the people" is "the very living source from which alone can come the correction of all the innate shortcomings of social institutions."[10]

Pro-capitalist writers have exaggerated Luxemburg's differences with Lenin. Indeed, one self-appointed editor of Luxemburg's work seems to have made it a life goal to misrepresent the two Marxist revolutionaries as "poles apart." This editor, Bertram D. Wolfe, even went so far as to re-title an influential article Luxemburg published in 1904. Instead of Luxemburg's title, "Organizational Questions of the Russian Social Democracy," Wolfe substituted what he called the more "attractive" title, "Leninism or Marxism?"[11] Luxemburg never contrasted Lenin to Marx the way Wolfe's title implies she did. (Indeed, in his introduction to this article, the worthy editor himself complained that "Her polemical tone is, for her, remarkably gentle.") Unfortunately, this sort of "scholarship" is not at all rare among many puffed-up professors who like to make a fuss about their own supposed objectivity.

The best antidote to this sort of misrepresentation is to read Rosa Luxemburg's writings for oneself. Judging from her own words, there is no question that she and Lenin shared their most basic views. She welcomed the October Revolution, and when it came to the most important issues of the day she sided with the Bolsheviks against the German party of which she was a member. Luxemburg and Lenin also happened to be personal friends. After her death, Lenin criticized the German Communists for not having published her collected works.

Like many original thinkers, of course, Luxemburg and Lenin had different opinions on a number of important issues. For example, Luxemburg's theory of imperialism, presented in her book *Accumulation of Capital*, is very different from the theory Lenin presented in *Imperialism: The Highest Stage of Capitalism*. Luxemburg's theory, which makes imperialism dependent on the exploitation of noncapitalist regions of the globe, is almost certainly wrong, whereas Lenin's has been confirmed time and again.

Luxemburg also criticized Lenin and the Bolsheviks for insisting that nations have the right to self-determination—that is, the right to decide for themselves whether or not they want a separate state of their own. In her "Junius Pamphlet" and elsewhere, she argued that in the era of imperialism the right of nations to self-determination could never be realized, and in the era of socialism it would be largely irrelevant. In response, however, Lenin argued that the right of nations to self-determination is a basic democratic right that Marxists should firmly support. Looking back, it is easy to see that Lenin's position on this question was much more in tune with national feelings in the twentieth century.

On some points, however, Luxemburg appears to have been right and Lenin wrong. Writing from her prison cell in 1918, she criticized the Bolsheviks for not allowing capitalists to vote and for restricting freedom of the press and the rights of association and assembly. Without "the most unlimited, the broadest democracy and public opinion," she said, "the rule of the broad mass of people is entirely unthinkable."[12]

At the same time, Luxemburg recognized that the fate of the Russian Revolution could have been much different if the revolution in Germany had been victorious. Over and over again she stressed the decisive importance of the revolution in Germany to the survival of the Bolshevik Revolution. Lenin shared this view. Unfortunately, the German revolution was defeated. Russia was left isolated, decimated by war and invaded by no fewer than twelve foreign armies.

In prison while World War I raged around her, Luxemburg wrote to a friend: "You know that, in spite of it all, I really hope to die at my post, in a street fight or in prison."[13] On January 15, 1919, she was arrested by soldiers of the German Federal Republic and murdered in cold blood, along with her comrade Karl Liebnecht. Born a few days before the Paris Commune, Rosa Luxemburg died at her post a little over a year after the Bolshevik Revolution.

Notes

1. Karl Marx, *Capital* Vol. 1 (New York: International Publishers, 1967), p. 44.

2. Karl Marx, *Capital* Vol. 1.

3. Money, by the way, is unique among commodities, in that the magnitude of its value does not necessarily depend on the amount of average, socially necessary labor time wrapped up in producing the coins or paper money.

4. Karl Marx, *Economic and Philosophic Manuscripts of 1844,* (New York: International Publishers, 1964); (New York: Prometheus Books, 1987). This work is sometimes referred to as the *Paris Manuscripts,* since Marx wrote it when he was living in exile in Paris.

5. Notably in the first chapter of *Capital* Vol. 1.

6. Refer to the list of further readings at the end of this chapter.

7. Translator's preface (Edward Fitzgerald) to Karl Mehring, *Karl Marx: The Story of His Life* (New York: Covici Fiede Publishers, 1935), p. viii.

8. V.I. Lenin, *Collected Works* Vol. 33 (Moscow: Progress Publishers, 1966), p. 210.

9. Karl Marx and Friedrich Engels, *Collected Works* Vol. 45 (New York: International Publishers, 1991), p. 408.

10. Rosa Luxemburg, *The Russian Revolution and Leninism or Marxism?* (Ann Arbor: University of Michigan Press, 1961), p. 62.

11. Bertram D. Wolfe, ed., Introduction to ibid., p. 15.
12. Ibid., p. 67.
13. Letter to Sonja Liebknecht from Wronte Prison, May 2, 1917. Reprinted in Stephen Eric Bronner, ed., *The Letters of Rosa Luxemburg* (Boulder: Westview Press, 1978), p. 203.

4

The Capitalist State and Ideology

The bourgeoisie has conquered for itself in the modern representative state exclusive political sway. The executive of the modern state is but a committee for managing the common affairs of the whole bourgeoisie.

—*The Communist Manifesto*

In Chapter 3 we took a quick look at economic practice in capitalist societies. By the end of Chapter 4, after we have touched on political and ideological practices, we will have a more complete picture of capitalist societies. The first section of this chapter focuses on the systems of institutions that account for by far the greater part of political practice in capitalist societies: the state. As we will see, in the course of discussing what modern capitalist states do, it will also be necessary to talk about ideological practice.

States and Ruling Classes

In communal societies, customs, habits, and traditions regulated social relations. If a member of a communal society violated these social practices, he or she was subject to direct punishment by any or all other members of the society. Tensions within communal societies might have existed for a long time because of the division of labor between males and females, the medicine man and other members of the tribe, or the young and the old. Nevertheless, as Walter Rodney pointed out with reference to African communal societies, these differences were not typically explosive, because they were not typically exploitative: The surplus product was not privately appropriated, and the women and children were not private property to be traded or disposed of at will.[1]

We've already learned that, as new forces of production appeared in some communal societies and it became possible to produce a social surplus, it also became possible to put captives to work as slaves and appropriate whatever they produced over what was necessary to keep them alive. With the new division of labor between slaves and non-slaves, social tensions greatly increased. The old communal system of ownership died, as the surplus product slaves produced fell into the hands of a smaller and smaller minority. This minority in turn used its control over the means of production to enslave an ever-larger number of people, whether they were captured in wars or born into slavery.

As the slave population grew in size, slave owners came to rely on other members of society, including some members of the slave class itself, to defend their privileges. Despite all the measures used to prevent organized rebellion, however, violent revolts did break out, pitting slaves against the slave owners' overseers and soldiers. With the outbreak of violent clashes between social classes and the threat of further clashes breaking out at any time, an entirely new social practice appeared: *political practice*. What is at stake in political practice, to put it in as few words as possible, is control of the surplus product of society. Which social group will be in control and thus define the general character of society as a whole?

Even from this very sketchy account we can see that, along with private ownership of the means of production, there also appeared a division of labor in the enforcement of social relations, particularly to keep the slaves in check. Instead of direct enforcement of customs by all members of the community themselves, a new specialized group arose that viewed itself as the final authority (or an instrument of divine authority) when it came to enforcing social relations, arbitrating conflicts, and defending the society against external attack. This small but organized group within a society was the beginning of the *state*.

In the previous example, we can see how the slave owners' ability to dominate society economically—that is, their economic power as a class—was tied to their state power. This is yet another illustration of just how interdependent social practices (in this case, economic and political practices) are. This simplified account also puts into sharp relief a point that is as true of modern capitalism as it was of ancient slave societies: The existence of a state is evidence of the existence of an exploiting class. When the various institutions of the state actually promote the interests of a particular class, that class is a *ruling class*.[2]

Not all exploiting classes are ruling classes, of course. We have already seen, for example, that capitalist merchants, manufacturers, and money lenders existed for a long time in medieval European societies dominated by feudal lords. Capitalists found themselves increasingly at odds with these lords, however, as long as the latter continued to promote feudal social relations that limited capital accumulation. The capitalists' profit motive set them in opposition to feudal property relations, Church authorities, feudal bonds tying a large part of the workforce to the countryside, and other limits placed on capital accumulation. The Crusades expanded trade with the Middle East and beyond and promoted the pillage of gold from the Western Hemisphere. These developments only brought the old relations of production promoted by feudal lords and the Church into greater and greater conflict with the new forces of production promoted by the rising capitalists.

The only way to freely develop the new forces of production and in that way to vastly increase capital accumulation was for the capitalists to challenge the monopoly of political power by feudal lords and the Church. These challenges took the form of violent revolutions first in England in 1640, then in France in 1789, and then elsewhere. The changes followed a pattern: In one case after another, a class that came to appropriate more and more of the social surplus rebelled against the old ruling class and sometimes succeeded in making its own representatives the political rulers of society. Having gained political power, the new ruling class used the institutions of the state to more or less rapidly transform social relations of production at the expense of the class that had just been overthrown.

Victorious capitalist classes lifted feudal obligations tying peasants to the countryside, confiscated church property, swept away the old guild system, abolished hereditary privileges, and so on. The impact of these revolutionary changes in turn was passed along every fiber of the netlike structure of society, transforming a whole range of legal, religious, moral, philosophical, scientific, and artistic practices and social relations. In this way, the new capitalist rulers to a large extent determined the character of the new society.

One conclusion we can draw from a survey of the histories of a great number of societies is that taken as a whole, every stable state has promoted some particular form of exploitation characteristic of one or another mode of production. In the case of the institutions of capitalist states, for example, they operate to ensure that social relations that promote private appropriation of surplus value are reproduced. Among the most visible state institutions that do this are police forces, armies, court systems, prisons, and other institutions that ruling classes rely on to put down direct challenges to their political authority. In addition to these institutions, capitalist rulers also have at their disposal secret police agencies, networks of spies and informants, organized strikebreakers, and other "secret weapons" for use in times of emergency.

Every state is composed in part of institutions that rely on violence and the threat of violence to divide and disorganize those who are ruled and in that way to ensure that one class continues to dominate others. These repressive institutions range from courts of law in the most democratic societies to death squads in the least democratic societies. When Engels referred to the state as "a group of armed men," he had in view a picture of the state as the totality of these repressive institutions of class rule.

Recognizing this, successful leaders of revolutionary classes have seldom simply "seized" or "taken over" the repressive state institutions of the rulers they've overthrown. On the contrary, they have almost always replaced the repressive state institutions of the overthrown class with new ones. These observations confirm Lenin's view in *The State and Revolution* that if a revolutionary class is to rise to state power it must destroy at least the most repressive institutions of the old state and build new and different institutions on their ashes.[3]

In modern capitalist societies, however, a class cannot retain state power by relying solely on repression. Once a revolutionary class has destroyed the old state institutions or made them over in its own image, its most active members need to dominate hostile classes and social groups allied with them, while at the same time leading their own class and its allies. Antonio Gramsci called the process of dominating class enemies and leading class allies *hegemony*. In order to achieve hegemony, Gramsci said, the most active spokespeople (or what he called the organic intellectuals) of the ruling class must spread their influence throughout society, to all social practices. Today, the struggle for hegemony remains an important flashpoint of class struggle in capitalist societies.

Gramsci's observations underscore the fact that modern capitalist states do lots of things besides repressing workers. In the United States, Germany, Japan, and other societies, for example, a wide range of national, local, and municipal institutions undertake hundreds of functions, from "national defense" to inspecting elevators. These capitalist states are complicated, and they require close, detailed study. For our purposes, however, we should notice at least three things.

First of all, we should recognize that conflicts between states are conflicts between ruling classes. Time and again in the twentieth century capitalist ruling classes have called on millions of workers to fight and die in wars, by appealing to God and Country, Freedom, Liberty, Democracy, or national defense. These emotional appeals to national interests have almost always concealed the fact that, to put it bluntly, the poor were expected to kill and to die for the sake of the rich. This point is perhaps well enough known to not need much more discussion here.

Second, we should consider the fact that capitalist states have funded public schools, libraries, post offices, roads, bridges, harbors, airports, and other projects that have benefited a large number of people, including workers. Capitalist lawmakers have passed laws regulating trusts, outlawing child labor, establishing maximum work hours and minimum wages, and setting up hundreds of other social programs. Furthermore, many capitalist governments have supported some measure of national health care, social security, unemployment insurance, and so on.

Does any of this compromise the Marxist view that capitalists and workers are hostile forces in society? To answer this question, we need to keep two points in mind that are important for an understanding of state power today.

First, just as it is a logical mistake to assume that what each individual soldier sees as his self-interest is necessarily the same as the goals of the army as a whole, so also it is a mistake to assume that the perceived interests of one or another individual capitalist are the same as the perceived interests of capitalists as a class. What Marx and Engels referred to as "the common affairs of the whole bourgeoisie"[4] may well be very different from the sum of their individual affairs. Individual capitalists may be interested in squeezing workers for everything they're worth; nevertheless, capitalists *as a class* have learned from bitter experience that if you kill the hen you will not get any more eggs. Unrestricted exploitation has led to strikes, labor violence, shrinking consumer markets, and at times even revolutionary upheaval. The North American tycoon Joseph Kennedy registered the danger when he said that he would prefer to give workers "a piece" rather than the "whole pie." This lesson became especially clear during the Great Depression of the 1930s, and since then "the executive of the modern state"[5] has increasingly concerned itself with state intervention in capitalist economies, including support of social programs.

State spending on social programs usually has, among other things, the identifiable function of promoting and at the same time hiding exploitation and inequality. Within capitalist societies, for example, public education appears at first to be egalitarian; nevertheless, it serves first and foremost as a publicly funded job training program for capitalist industry. Seen in this light, public education is an important means of ensuring ruling class hegemony. Similarly, hundreds of other "social programs," which may genuinely provide some immediate benefit to workers, provide far more benefits to the biggest capitalists. These include the postal service, fire departments, and national health insurance.

Furthermore, much state spending on "public works" is little more than public funding to provide expensive and unprofitable facilities (such as railroads, highways, harbors, mass transit systems, and so on) to private industries. In Chapter 5 we'll touch on the related issue of the role of military spending in many modern capitalist economies.

Second, it is important to recognize that the achievements that working people and others enjoy—achievements such as the right of workers to unionize, child labor legislation, the right of women to vote, minimum wage laws, social security and civil rights laws—were not the gifts of softhearted capitalists and lawmakers who have gradually come to see the light. On the contrary, they were hard-won concessions wrought from capitalist rulers in the face of vicious opposition. Strike leader Elizabeth Gurley Flynn summarized U.S. labor history as follows: "Struggles—for a few cents more an hour, for a few minutes less work a day—were long and bitterly fought. Nothing was handed on a silver platter to the American working class by employers. All their hard-won gains came through their own efforts and solidarity."[6]

The truth of Flynn's observation has been borne out in recent years, as employers, aided and abetted by the state, have attacked U.S. labor unions, and as wages and benefits have plummeted. Workers have discovered over and over again that a factory owner who has suffered a temporary defeat in a strike does not for all that cease to be a factory owner. And similarly, a capitalist state does not lose its class character just because, for reasons of farsightedness or in order to cut its losses in the face of working-class solidarity, capitalist rulers meet one or another demand of workers.

The third and final point we'll make regarding the function of institutions of the state has to do with the following fact: Some state institutions such as city councils, local governments, and even ministries at the national level can be delivered into the hands of one class, whereas state power as a whole remains in the hands of the old ruling class. In India, Italy, and elsewhere, for example, regional and city governments have been controlled by Communists for years.

Marx, Engels, Lenin, Luxemburg, and Gramsci, focusing on a variety of different cases, each had something to say about the question of Marxist involvement in governments of capitalist states. More recent historical materialist researchers have conducted important work on this subject, too. They have pointed out that in some cases political systems have been set up in such a manner as to allow working-class control of some institutions of the state without endangering capitalist-class rule on the national level. Furthermore, in other cases when working-class leaders have successfully fought the uphill battle to gain high office legally, real decisionmaking power has shifted away from that office or ministry to other state institutions firmly under capitalist control.

And finally, we need to reflect on the fact that capitalists who have faced legal, democratic, and peaceful challenges to their exclusive political sway have time and again violated their own constitutions to overturn elections and call troops into the streets to maintain their class rule by brute force.

Ideology

We have already seen that every state is, in part at least, "organized oppression." As Gramsci emphasized, however, no state can secure the rule of one class over others by violence and threats of violence alone. In addition to resorting to violence and fear, states also determine the way members of societies act even when they are not forced against their will to act a certain way. Even in states as outrageously repressive as Hitler's Germany, Pinochet's Chile, the Republic of South Africa under apartheid, or contemporary Guatemala, state power resides not only in coercion but also (at least to some extent) in the consent of many if not most of those who are ruled. Gramsci's point is especially important, however, when it comes to more democratic capitalist states such as the United States, Japan, and Germany.

One of the most obvious ways in which ruling classes have gained the consent of those they rule is through religion. It is not too difficult to recognize that the religions favored by ruling classes have tended to portray God (the highest "master," "lord," or "king") as a larger-than-life copy of the rulers. Today, although few capitalist countries still have state churches, God is often portrayed as an idealized capitalist boss, promoting the faithful and "firing" the unrepentant. In this and other ways religious practices have encouraged people to imagine that existing social relations are eternal, essentially just, and the best that can be hoped for.[7]

What is less obvious, perhaps, is that law as well as the prevailing morality, philosophy, art, education, and entertainment also guarantee the consent of the governed in much the same way religions do. We have already seen, for example, that when they overthrew the old feudal rulers, capitalists replaced the feudal system of customary obligations and privileges with new legal codes that promoted social relations of production conducive to private appropriation of surplus value. These legal practices could not operate openly in a class-biased manner, however, at the risk of ceasing to guarantee the consent of workers and others. When social groups no longer recognize laws as "theirs," they fail to obey them unless they are forced to do so.

This helps to explain why framers of bourgeois constitutions have put so much emphasis on the *equality* of all citizens before the law ("justice is blind") and on equal representation in elections ("one person one vote"). By emphasizing equality, bourgeois political thinkers have helped create the impression that every member of society, exploiter and exploited alike, has an equal stake in the continuity of the state. This very limited equality, however, conceals a much broader reality of class domination and exploitation. The French writer Anatole France summed up the supposed neutrality of even the most democratic capitalist states as follows: "The bourgeois state," he said, "forbids with the same majesty the rich as well as the poor from sleeping under bridges."[8]

Similar remarks could be made with reference to morality, philosophy, art, education, and entertainment. To confirm this, one need only judge for oneself to what extent the corporate-owned press and the film and television industries—not to mention public school courses stressing "citizenship skills"—promote the sanctity of private property, uncritical respect for authority, and other sacred themes of bourgeois morality.

Evidently, laws, morality, philosophy, art, education, entertainment, and other elements of the "superstructure" in capitalist societies overwhelmingly promote capitalist relations of production. Furthermore, these elements appear to do so mainly by affecting the way people behave even when they are not forced against their will to act one way or another. To cite one example: After decades of vilifying Arab people, the corporate-owned news and entertainment media in the United States has made it popularly acceptable to target Arab civilians for attack, to ensure western control over Middle East oil.

Each of the various legal, religious, moral, philosophical, educational, recreational, and artistic practices that promotes dominant social relations is an *ideology*. As we will see presently, religious, moral, philosophical, recreational, or artistic practices that oppose dominant social relations are also ideologies. Taken together, all of these practices that promote or oppose dominant social relations make up the ideological practice of a society.

Sometimes the word *ideology* is used by non-Marxists to mean any bad or wrong idea. In the past, even many Marxists have defined ideology as "false consciousness." In reality, however, no particular belief within an ideological system is necessarily false. Some of the worst Cold War propaganda reports of corruption and incompetence in the Soviet Union, for example, happen to have been true. What is false, however, is the common assumption in the West that the fall of the Soviet Union proves that socialism can never work. This assumption serves the further ideological function of assuring an audience—usually without explicitly saying so—that capitalism is the best of all possible social arrangements.

To take another example, let's consider the rather common claim that the U.S. political system is democratic. The problem with this claim is not that it is false. After all, even in view of the extremely limited and biased character of representative democracy in the United States, the fact remains that elections take place on the basis of one person one vote, and candidates who win a majority of the votes take office. Nevertheless, the claim does not even come close to being an accurate description of the U.S. political system over all, because it glosses over such realities as class rule, state repression, and ideological hegemony—and, as we will see in Chapter 5, it ignores the fact that the social stability that makes representative democracy possible within the borders of the United States has been purchased in large part at the price of massive exploitation and tyranny outside its borders. To describe the U.S. political system by focusing only on formal features such as multiparty elections—even when the description is made up only of true statements—is narrow, one-sided, and therefore misleading. The result is half-truths. As strange as it may sound to those of us who have received our schooling in capitalist countries, Marx opposed this sort of one-sided thinking.

This example illustrates the fact that an ideology is characterized not only by what it points to as important, or what it brings to our attention, but also by what it ignores, hides, or directs our attention *away from,* or what it pronounces to be unimportant or impossible. By carefully selecting only those facts that confirm one's view and ignoring all evidence for opposing views, it is possible to make a case for even the most skewed prejudices. Exploitation and the gap between the rich and the poor, to take only two examples, are realities that pro-capitalist writers, professors, and politicians seldom talk about.

Another typical feature of ideology is the assumption that there is no such a thing as ideology. This assumption, it seems, is shared by most writers and professors who make their livings precisely by promoting ruling-class ideologies!

There is another reason why defining ideology as "false consciousness" is misleading: Historical materialists do not view ideology primarily as the result of conscious planning or conspiracies on the part of cynical politicians and bosses. Rather, they hold that ideology for the most part operates behind the backs of both workers and capitalists, as they live their lives from day to day. Men and women routinely perform the tasks assigned them by the division of labor, the relations of production, law and customary morality without being forced to do so. Every day, we obey laws even when no police officer is in sight and we follow established work rules even when the boss is on vacation. Ideology is present in the conduct of individuals in families as well as their behavior toward other members of society, their attitudes toward nature, their judgment on the meaning of life in general, and their obedience to God, the State, the Party, Law, Justice, Truth, and all the other real and imaginary authorities we spell with capital letters. Indeed, ideology is so much present in all the deeds of individuals that it defines to a large extent how members of a society view each other and how they view themselves.

Thus, ideology takes us in a circle: Every time we obey a law or an authority we reproduce existing social relations; and by doing this, we in turn reproduce or "recognize" ourselves as law-abiding citizens, religious believers, members of one or another nation or race, party members, members of the "middle class," and so on.

This, of course, is not to say that all laws and authority should or even can be done away with. Rather, it is a description of how social relations are reproduced in a society and a deeper insight into ourselves as the "ensemble of social relations."[9]

Although ideology takes us in a circle, it is important to recognize that it is not an unbreakable circle: Ideological practices do not always just qualify people for the roles they have been assigned by the division of labor and the mode of production. If this were so, it would not be possible to explain most historical change, because it would remain a mystery how individuals and classes could ever rise against existing relations of production and change them. As we all know, however, in certain circumstances members of one or another social group have in fact rejected relations of exploitation as well as ruling class ideologies and have adopted ideologies of protest and rebellion.

This takes us back to a point discussed in an earlier chapter: Marxism does not deny that law, religion, morality, and art have an influence on history and society. On the contrary, many Marxists stress the important role revolutionary ideologies have played down through the centuries. At the same time, however, they maintain that changes that have taken place in economic practices have influenced changes in law, religion, morality, philosophy, and art much more than vice versa.

Is the Concept of a Ruling Class Obsolete?

But what about the claims so often repeated these days that there are no ruling classes in modern capitalist societies? The only way to answer this question is to investigate particular cases. Since so many voices in the West repeat the claim that the United States is a pluralistic society without a ruling class—and since so many people in eastern Europe and elsewhere evidently believe this claim these days—it makes sense to turn our attention to the case of the United States. In the course of doing this, we might also gain a firmer grasp of what has already been said regarding the state and ideology.

In Chapter 2 we considered some of the abundant evidence that the United States is a deeply divided class society. We saw that, roughly speaking, the 1.25 million superrich in the United States make up a class of big capitalists, which we called big business. But what evidence is there that big business is a ruling class? Before we try to answer this question, we need to consider how we would go about recognizing a ruling class if we "saw" one.

Earlier in this chapter we learned that when the institutions of a state promote the interests of a class considered as a whole, that class is a ruling class. Drawing from what has already been said, then, the first step in establishing that big business is a ruling class would be to establish that, on the whole, dominant political institutions in the United States promote the political and economic power of big business.

At the outset, however, we encounter an objection: Some opponents of Marxism deny that institutions of the state can promote the interests of big business or any other class, because, they say, members of classes do not come together to define what their common interests are. We will return to this objection presently. First, however, we should note that, according to this account, society (or as it is sometimes called in these discussions, "civil society") is a mosaic of competing private interests, some of which come together from time to time to form coalitions, often across class lines, to pursue their private goals. Meanwhile, the state for its part is said to stand above all of these competing interests, to represent the higher interests of society as a whole.

The problem with this account is that it ignores some very important social realities that do not fit its assumptions. The fact that economic and political practices are so interdependent, for example, throws into doubt the notion of "civil society" as a field of competition that is separate from political struggles; moreover, the existence of exploitation and class conflict throw into doubt the notion of "higher interests of society as a whole." By ignoring or dismissing these and other considerations, mainstream social scientists save themselves the embarrassment of acknowledging the reality of capitalist political power.

If I had the space I could launch into a long discussion of state policies in the United States and how these policies promote private appropriation of surplus value, the unity of big business as a class, the supremacy of U.S. capitalism in the global market, and so on. On the domestic front, I could discuss such things as tax policy, protectionism, and state subsidies to industry and agribusiness. I could also survey the history of labor reform and discover a tight correlation between grassroots militancy and the reforms that followed. Or I could examine long-standing inequalities in public education and the consistently pro-capitalist bias of teaching materials. Turning to foreign policy, I could investigate the connection between the demands of big business and actual U.S. foreign policy decisions. Or I could examine the content of the corporate-owned media and entertainment industries, relating them to specific goals of policy planners at the national level.

Of course, I don't have the space here to do any of these things. If I did, however, and if readers were to take the time to familiarize themselves with a wide range of research conducted by Marxists and non-Marxists alike, what would emerge is a broad pattern linking the policies of U.S. state institutions on the one hand with the perceived interests of big business on the other.

Accepting that there is a consistent correlation between state policies and the interests of big business, however, the following question arises: How does big business determine what its class interests are, and how does it use state institutions to promote these interests?

First we should note that the vast majority of the "string-pullers" in the United States represent big business. With few exceptions, the most influential government officials and the highest ranking legislators and politicians of both the Democratic and Republican Parties belong to one of two categories: (1) high-level executives of major corporations, partners in major law firms, landowners, and financial tycoons; or else (2) lawyers, bank managers, professors, army officers, and other faithful and well-paid servants of the people in the first category. There are individual exceptions, of course, and these exceptions are often cited as proof of the pluralism of capitalist societies. Nevertheless, the exceptions are conspicuously rare and their influence on state policies at the national level has been negligible.

In his book, *A People's History of the United States,* historian Howard Zinn quoted from a report prepared in 1976 by a group of intellectuals and political leaders from Japan, the United States, and Western Europe:

> To the extent that the United States was governed by anyone during the decades after World War II, it was governed by the President acting with the support and cooperation of key individuals and groups in the executive office, the federal bureaucracy, Congress, and the more important businesses, banks, law firms, foundations, and media, which constitute the private sector's "Establishment."[10]

The author of this part of the report, a Harvard professor named Samuel Huntington, went on to say

> The day after his election, the size of [the President's] majority is almost—if not entirely—irrelevant to his ability to govern the country. What counts then is his ability to mobilize support from the leaders of key institutions in a society and government. . . . This coalition must include key people in Congress, the executive branch, and the private-sector "Establishment."[11]

The members of the coalition that professor Huntington described act in accordance with the recommendations of certain advisors and public and private institutions related in one way or another to what Huntington called the "private-sector 'Establishment,'" or what we have been calling big business. There are thousands of people employed to identify what the collective interests of big business are. These include the 1,300 members of the Council on Foreign Relations as well as the Committee on Economic Development, the Urban Land Institute, the Trilateral Commission, and other public and private commissions, policy planning institutes, and think tanks. What's more, regional and national legislatures also function in large part to fulfill this role.

Once the interests of big business have been identified, a number of institutions ensure that state policies reflect these interests. Among these institutions we may mention the two-party political system in the United States, hundreds of lobbies representing big business interests in regional and national capitals, and the corporate-owned news and entertainment industries. These and other institutions efficiently guarantee an unbroken connection between big business and the highest levels of government and other state institutions. This connection is well-documented and widely accepted today, even by non-Marxist experts.

Unlike most mainstream political scientists, however, few Marxists assume without argument that this arrangement is beneficial to both workers and capitalists alike. And because most if not all Marxists reject this assumption, they are in a better position to recognize that in the United States, rule *over* the majority is disguised as rule *of* the majority.

At the same time, however, it is far-fetched to view class rule as a result of a giant conspiracy in which politicians secretly uphold the interests of rulers behind a smoke screen of lies. As we know by now, Marx emphasized over and over again that social relations are not usually the result of a conscious plan. Because of this, and because they demand that explanations of historical change draw strong causal connections, historical materialists are typically very skeptical of conspiracy theories.

So far, we have established a connection between what big business sees as its interests and what state institutions actually do. Now, if this connection can be cut, at least with reference to the most important institutions of a state, by actions that the state itself encourages (such as voting), then this would count as evidence against the existence of a ruling class.

Applying this test to one case after another in which democratic processes have threatened capitalist-class rule, however, the overwhelming evidence confirms the Marxist account of state power: Time and again the decisions of democratically elected officials have been quietly squelched when they have come into conflict with capitalist interests. Recognizing this, Edmund Morgan noted in his book *Inventing the People* that participation in elections was "a legitimizing ritual, a rite by which the populace renewed their consent to an oligarchical power structure."[12]

Thus, representative democracy in the United States is actually more a means of maintaining ruling-class hegemony than a means of ensuring that the majority has a voice in government. Furthermore, the largely unreported history of the United States—from the Palmer raids of 1920 right down to the surveillance activities of the FBI and other agencies today—contains many examples of massive state repression against U.S. citizens on behalf of big business.

Consciously or not, many people in the United States react against the state as a hostile power imposed upon them from above. This is reflected in the low voter turnout for elections as well as widespread cynicism summed up by the saying that if voting could change things, it would be illegal. Reaction against the state as a hostile power is also reflected in a wide array of "alienated" behavior including tax dodging, alcoholism, drug abuse, religious escapism, racism, and ever-increasing violence in the streets.

I have suggested that the policies of state institutions in the United States have overwhelmingly promoted the interests of big business. I have identified some of the mechanisms that at any given time connect state policies of the United States with the perceived interests of big business. And finally, I have pointed to evidence that the system of representative democracy in the United States makes it difficult for any significant challenge to be mounted through legal means against the exclusive political sway of big business. In view of all of this, it is reasonable to conclude that there is indeed a ruling class in the United States. So far, I have called this ruling class big business. In Chapter 5, as we take another look at it from a different angle, we'll consider a more accurate name for this ruling class.

Summary

Key terms discussed in this chapter include *political practice, state, ruling class, hegemony,* and *ideology.*

As Engels noted, the very existence of a state is itself a demonstration that a society is deeply divided along class lines. Although leaders of most modern states pretend to represent the interests of society as a whole, no state ever really does. A state always stands against part of society, whether it be the slave class, feudal serfs, peasants, wage laborers, or some other class. Stated in even fewer words, a state is always a class state.

The institutions of a state always promote certain social relations that characterize one or another mode of production. When institutions of a state on the whole promote a particular form of exploitation, then the exploiting class qualifies as a ruling class.

In the more industrialized capitalist countries, class rule is never limited exclusively to domination by force. A ruling class can retain state power only if it leads its allies and dominates those it exploits. Gramsci called this process of leading class allies and dominating class enemies hegemony. Part of this process of hegemony involves manipulating the way people act even when they are not directly forced to act a certain way.

All of the various legal, religious, moral, philosophical, recreational, and artistic practices that either promote or oppose dominant social relations are ideologies. Taken together, all of these practices make up the ideological practice of a society.

Big business is not only the economically dominant class in the United States, it is also the politically dominant class—the ruling class. The institutions of the state promote big business's agenda, quite often to the detriment of other classes.

Reading List

Engels, Friedrich. *The Origin of the Family, Private Property and the State.* New York: International Publishers, 1972. This book is a good place to begin a study of the state. Although much of the anthropological discussion has become outdated, Engels's most important and original claims have generally been verified by more recent researchers.

Gramsci, Antonio. *State and Civil Society* (pp. 210–276 of *Selections from the Prison Notebooks*). New York: International Publishers, 1971.

*Lenin, V.I. *The State and Revolution.* Several editions by different publishers. Unfortunately, Lenin did not distinguish strongly enough in this book between undemocratic states such as that of Russia at the turn of the century and the democratic capitalist states of western Europe. Gramsci's political writings help to compensate for this shortcoming.

Luxemburg, Rosa ("Junius"). *The Russian Revolution.* Several editions by different publishers. This text first appeared in 1919. Refer to my comments on the "Junius Pamphlet" in the segment on Luxemburg at the end of Chapter 3.

*Marx, Karl. *The Eighteenth Brumaire of Louis Bonaparte.* Published in various collections. Engels called Marx's account of the rise to power of Louis Napoleon in France the epitome of the materialist conception of history. This writing from 1852 is an exemplary historical analysis that shows why and how "every class struggle is a political struggle."

_____. *The Civil War in France.* New York: International Publishers, 1940. Marx's examination of the failures, achievements, and promises of the Paris Commune. (Refer to the "Paris Commune" entry in the glossary.)

*Antonio Gramsci
(1891–1937)*

Founders of Historical Materialism

Antonio Gramsci was born the son of a poor clerk and a working mother on the island of Sardinia off the coast of Italy. In his early twenties he was a Socialist Party organizer in Italy, and later he became one of the founders of the Communist Party of Italy and a member of the Italian parliament. In 1926 he was arrested by Mussolini's fascist police on trumped-up charges. During his trial, the prosecutor pointed to Gramsci and said: "We must stop this brain working for twenty years!"[13] Sure enough, he received a twenty-year prison sentence, which he did not survive. Lack of light, fresh air, and adequate food and medical care took its toll on Gramsci, who had been a hunchback since childhood and had suffered from a number of other illnesses. After ten painful years in fascist prisons, Gramsci died.

Although the fascists succeeded in imprisoning Gramsci, they did not stop his brain from working. Thanks to his own tremendous "optimism of the will,"[14] he produced several thousand pages of profound writing on politics and culture. These notebooks were written under the eye of prison censors and smuggled out of prison. *Selections from the Prison Notebooks* (published by International Publishers in 1971) includes his writings on the study of history, the role of intellectuals in society, and his influential political essays

"State and Civil Society" and "The Modern Prince." It also includes an excellent introduction by the editors, sketching out the historical and personal background of these writings.

Gramsci contributed greatly to our understanding of how capitalists rule by consent in industrialized countries with democractic traditions. For this reason, his writings are very important today.

* * *

Perhaps Gramsci himself has provided the most inspiring insight into his life, in the form of his published letters from prison. Some of these letters have been collected and edited by Lynne Lawner and published (by Noonday Press in 1973) under the title *Letters from Prison: Antonio Gramsci.*

Notes

1. Walter Rodney, *How Europe Underdeveloped Africa* (Washington, D.C.: Howard University Press, 1974), pp. 36–37 and 39.

2. The interests of an exploiting class as a whole presumably include continuing to appropriate a great part of the social surplus, whereas the interests of an exploited class include the mitigation of its exploitation.

3. Lenin, of course, was referring to genuine social revolutions, not palace coups pitting one faction of a ruling class or group against a different faction of the same class or group.

4. David McLellan, ed., *Karl Marx: Selected Writings* (Oxford: Oxford University Press, 1977), p. 223.

5. David McLellan, ed., *Karl Marx: Selected Writings.*

6. Elizabeth Gurley Flynn, *The Rebel Girl* (New York: International Publishers, 1973), p. 21.

7. At the same time, important twentieth-century liberation movements have emphasized egalitarian and revolutionary aspects of Christianity, Islam, Buddhism, and other religions. The relationship between religions and class struggle is a complex topic, which only recently has been receiving the attention it deserves from Marxists.

8. Quoted in Karl Korsch, *Karl Marx* (New York: Russell and Russell, 1938), p. 142.

9. McLellan, ed., *Karl Marx,* p. 157. The study of this aspect of ideological practice, which some Marxists refer to as "the constitution of the subject," is yet another area of historical materialism that until recently has remained almost entirely undeveloped.

10. Howard Zinn, *A People's History of the United States* (New York: Harper, 1980), p. 547.

11. Quoted in Zinn, *People's History,* pp. 547–548.

12. Edmund Morgan, *Inventing the People: The Rise of Popular Sovereignty in England and America* (New York: W. W. Norton and Company, 1988), p. 206.

13. Quoted by Quintin Hoare and Geoffrey N. Smith in their Introduction to Antonio Gramsci, *Selections from the Prison Notebooks* (New York: International Publishers, 1971), p. xviii.

14. Refer to Gramsci, *Selections,* p. 175, note 75.

5

Imperialism

Lenin was virtually prophetic, because as the colonial age advanced it became more and more obvious that those who stood to benefit most were the monopoly concerns, and especially those involved in finance.

—*Walter Rodney*

Capitalism today is very different from what it was two hundred years ago. In this chapter we'll take a look at some of the most important differences.

The Monopoly Stage of Capitalism

Ever since there have been capitalists, they have competed with each other for buyers. One of the chief ways to attract buyers is to offer commodities for sale at a lower price than one's rivals. For obvious reasons, large-scale producers can sell more cheaply than small-scale producers. Bigger producers can purchase raw materials more cheaply by buying in bulk, of course. And because they have more capital at their disposal to update machinery and invest in new production techniques than do their smaller rivals, large-scale producers can increase the productivity of labor, enabling fewer workers to produce more in less time. Big capitalists can also get credit more easily and on better terms than their smaller rivals, and they enjoy a number of other advantages including the ability to capture a larger share of the market through extensive advertising. Furthermore, some fields of modern industry—steel production, the construction of locomotives, shipbuilding, and so on—are quite impossible for small manufacturers to compete in.

As we can see, then, competition among industrial capitalists favors large producers over smaller ones. The same thing holds for agriculture, although at a much slower pace than in heavy industry. Many small farmers cannot afford to invest in heavy machinery, irrigation systems, fertilizers, pesticides, and improved seed stock. Furthermore, heavy machinery and other innovations can be put to use most efficiently when large areas of land are under cultivation. As a result, agricultural production has become more capital intensive—that is, the expenditure for what in Chapter 3 we called constant capital (capital expended for the means of production) has increased greatly relative to variable capital (capital expended for labor-power).

As large-scale machine production has been introduced into industry and agriculture to reduce the cost of production, more and more workers and small farmers have been replaced by labor-saving machinery. They, together with smaller capitalists who have been ruined by larger capitalists, have been pushed down into the ranks of wage earners. Small-business owners, highly paid professionals, self-employed artisans, and other members of the middle classes continue to make up an important part of industrialized capitalist societies, of course. This is why an analysis of the class makeup of these societies is not a simple matter and must be undertaken carefully, in detail and on a case-by-case basis. Nevertheless, there has been a marked tendency for these societies to "shake out" into a big working class and a much smaller capitalist class.

Over the years, the scale of production in one branch of industry after another has grown larger and larger, as big capitalists have ruined small ones. Hundreds and sometimes even thousands of workers in England, the United States, Germany, Japan, France, and elsewhere were brought together under one roof in steel foundries, coal mines, textile mills, and shipbuilding yards to operate larger and ever more complicated machines. The division of labor within a factory became much more complicated, as each step in the production process was undertaken by a different worker. Moreover, the division of labor within society as a whole also became much more complicated, as raw materials and parts were produced in one place and worked up or assembled hundreds, or even thousands of miles away. As a result, large numbers of workers were brought into connection and interdependence with one another. In this sense, capitalism collectivized production.

Capitalism has also collectivized the task of directing large capitalist firms. Increasingly, management responsibilities have been taken out of the hands of individual capitalists and put in the hands of highly paid professional management teams.

Meanwhile, in one branch of industry after another we have seen fewer and fewer capitalist firms producing on an ever-larger scale. The process that leads to an ever-larger scale of industry in fewer and fewer hands is called *concentration of production*. The growth of industry has gone hand in hand with concentration of production.

Technical innovations such as the steam engine, the cotton gin, and more recently, electronics, computers, and telecommunications technologies have made it possible to greatly increase the productivity of labor. Contrary to the technological determinists'[1] view of things, however, the relationship between technological innovation and economic development is not a one-way street running from the former to the latter. Improved technology is both a cause of concentration of production and a result of it. In an effort to increase the productivity of labor and in that way to increase the rate of exploitation, for instance, capitalist firms bought patents for new inventions and founded laboratories and research institutes. In this way, technological innovation and improvement have also been collectivized, along with other fields of economic production.

In one branch of industry after another competition has taken place among fewer but larger competitors. In conformity with the profit motive, capitalists strive to increase their capital, to add to existing capital part of the surplus value they have extracted from workers. As capital increases, production must extend. At the same time, bigger capitalists also increase their capital by wrenching capital from the hands of smaller capitalists. As a result, more and more capital ends up in the hands of fewer and fewer big capitalists. The process whereby ever-larger sums of capital come to be held in an ever-smaller number of hands is termed *concentration of capital*.

If a company is to survive in a field of large-scale production, it needs to control or command a lot of capital, to expand production, hold goods off the market for the best prices, improve machinery, and so on. Without command of ever-larger amounts of capital, a company would be one of the doomed small fish. Because of this need for ever more capital, individually owned capitalist companies have given way more and more to joint-stock companies, or corporations. As we might have suspected from our short discussion of joint-stock ownership in Chapter 2, this system allowed the biggest capitalists efficiently to collect large amounts of money capital under their control, making it possible for them to make a larger number of investments. One way this is done is by means of holding companies—that is, companies holding large blocks of shares in a number of different corporations.

As Marx foresaw in *Capital*, the concentration of production and capital has proceeded on an enormous scale in one branch of industry after another. In the last decades of the nineteenth century, concentration developed to such a degree that it resulted in the formation of monopolies, which began to play a decisive role in the economic life of the most highly industrialized societies. (By the way, when we speak of the formation of monopolies, we do not usually mean the domination of a market or branch of industry by just one company, but by a small number of companies or groups of companies.) Concentration of production leads to the formation of monopolies in whole spheres of industry. For example, as early as 1900, monopolies in the United States already held 50 percent of textile production in their hands, 54 percent of glass production, 60 percent of paper production, 84 percent of iron and steel production, and 81 percent of chemical production. Ever since then these percentages have steadily risen. Taking these trends into account, Lenin concluded that the turn of the twentieth century marked a breaking point between two very different forms of capitalism: the older competitive or free exchange capitalism and a new form of capitalism, which he called *monopoly capitalism*.

Once a few big companies dominate a particular branch of industry, they are in a position to fix production quotas, divide the market among themselves, and set prices above levels that would prevail under conditions of free competition. Throughout the twentieth century we have seen that companies have come together to form cartels and trusts to do just this. Other ways in which a group of capitalists may succeed in establishing a monopoly include combines, trade associations, and price agreements. Monopolies suppress competition in a number of ways including stopping supplies of raw materials, agreeing with unions to stop the supply of labor, cutting off deliveries, closing trade outlets, entering into exclusive purchase agreements with buyers, stopping credit, and selling below production costs to force competitors out of business.

Increasingly, monopolies expand vertically, to several related branches of production at once, in order to control the whole process of production of a line of goods, from the source of raw materials to the display shelf. Thus, a tire manufacturer may acquire chemical factories and rubber tree groves as well as retail tire stores. Other monopolies expand horizontally, to any of a number of unrelated fields of economic activity.

To get an idea of the scale of monopolies today, let's take a quick look at International Telephone and Telegraph (or ITT). This single diversified corporation, or conglomerate, owns firms that produce electronic components, lighting fixtures, microwave equipment, and semiconductors as well as aerospace, avionics, and navigations systems. ITT also owns companies that produce frozen foods, baked goods, candies, processed meat, silica, glass, tools and machine parts, heating and air conditioning systems, pumps, and fire protection equipment. ITT owns insurance companies, real estate and development companies, trade schools, research facilities, marketing and advertising companies, data services, credit and securities corporations, financial services, cable television systems, radio, telephone and telecommunications systems, restaurants, vending machine companies, shopping centers, wood preserves, mines, automobile and truck rental companies, parking garages, hotels, motels, and lots and lots of other companies in over fifty countries, from Argentina to Zambia.

This scale of concentration could never have taken place if capitalists allowed their money to lie idle until they had need of it, say for expansion of a plant or upgrading facilities. Capitalists must find sellers for their commodities quickly, they must have money capital ready at hand for the purchase of new raw materials at the right time, they must invest promptly and profitably the money they receive from sales, and they must keep abreast of technological innovations. If capitalists fail to do these things, they risk falling behind their competitors or being driven out of business. Furthermore, capitalists must respond quickly to changing market conditions to produce commodities for which there is an effective demand or for which a need can be produced by expanding the market through advertising or in some other way. Otherwise, the surplus value contained in the unsold commodities will be lost. From this review we can see that capitalists have a constant need for capital in the form of money.

Responding to this need, individual capitalists join together, thanks to the credit system and the banks, to advance each other the money they need to ensure that production and sale of commodities take place without interruption. Capitalists put their money in banks, and banks invest capital in industry.

In the course of running a current account for a company, however, a bank finds itself in a position to keep track of the company and control it by selectively extending or denying loans, lending at high or low interest rates, and so forth. As a result, industry has become dependent on the banks, which in many cases can make or break a company. Eventually, the banks' agents are appointed directors of trusts, corporations, and other companies. In this way one large bank may unite many companies by supplying them all with money capital to convert into industrial capital. As a result, banks today have at their command most of the money capital of all capitalists.

When banking capital merges with industrial capital and dominates it in this manner, the result is *finance capital*. During the course of the past hundred years, as I have indicated, and as Lenin observed as early as 1916, a small group of finance capitalists have concentrated control over much of the economic system in their hands and in this way have come to dominate society as a whole. It would be more accurate, therefore, to describe the ruling class of the United States and other highly industrialized capitalist societies as the finance capitalist class or monopoly capital, rather than big business, as we have been calling it so far.

The International Capitalist System

We have already seen that competition among capitalists leads to monopoly. As we will see somewhat later on, monopolies tend to spill over the borders of any single state. Let's back up for a moment to see how this tendency developed.

Throughout most of the eighteenth and nineteenth centuries, Great Britain was the undisputed industrial power, the "workshop of the world." Moreover, with its colonies in North America, India, Africa, Australia, and elsewhere, Great Britain was a colonial power without rivals. By the late nineteenth century, however, this situation began to change. Protecting themselves with tariff walls against British imports, Germany, the United States, and France developed into major capitalist powers in their own right. As the younger capitalist powers began to challenge Great Britain's leadership in industry, they also began to challenge it as the leading colonial power. Great

Britain and the other "Great Powers" became locked in a fierce competition for cheap sources of raw materials, new opportunities for capital investment, and new markets for manufactured goods.

For Great Britain, the most extensive colonial conquests in the period of monopoly capitalism took place between 1860 and 1880. For France and Germany, the main grab for colonies took place between 1880 and 1900. These and the other "Great Powers" shuffled and reshuffled alliances, carved up whole continents and skirmished with each other over economic spheres of interest. Between 1870 and 1890, for example, what has been called the "Scramble for Africa" reached its peak: In 1876 one-tenth of African territory was colonized by European powers; by 1900 nine-tenths of the continent had been colonized. In order to safeguard their domination over colonial lands, the "Great Powers" built up their armies and navies and set up military bases to watch over trade routes, force open new markets, and grab up new colonial lands. In the course of doing this they destroyed native societies, stripped the land of raw materials, imposed regimes of mass terror, and reduced tens of millions of people to worse misery than they had ever known.

In trade, the "Great Powers" were (and still are) able to exchange the products of a few hours of labor-time for the products of many more hours of labor-time in less industrialized societies of Asia, Africa, Latin America, and elsewhere. Recognizing the advantages, the "Great Powers" grabbed up territories not already colonized and set up huge plantations, farms, mines, railroads, harbors, and drilling rigs throughout these lands. By exporting the building materials, machinery, parts, and other capital necessary to set production into motion and keep it in motion, the colonial powers could then recruit local workers to perform the dirtiest, hardest, and most dangerous work at wages far below those of the home country. And to ensure that labor-power remained cheap in these lands, these same "Great Powers" kept wages and standards of living low. In some cases, as we know, workers in the colonized lands were (and still are) paid little more than enough to keep them alive. In this way, exporting capital to colonies allowed the "Great Power" capitalists to reap superprofits, or profits over and above what capitalists squeeze out of workers in the wealthier capitalist societies.[2]

This was the background for a new form of colonialism that relied on the export of capital, rather than just commodities, as in the past. As it turned out, however, the export of capital brought along its own problems. Capital exported obviously creates more capital. Exported capital in the form of mining equipment, for example, enables capitalists to turn coal into capital. This new capital then seeks profitable new investment, as fuel for steam engines, furnaces, and so forth. At the same time, however, the field for such investment is narrowed, because competition among the "Great Powers" narrows effective demand: Major markets, for instance, may be closed off to coal from competing monopoly groups, while at the same time the home market is glutted.

With more and more capital and fewer opportunities to invest it, the struggle among groups of monopolies seeking to extend their markets and spheres of operation took a fierce turn at the beginning of the twentieth century. These monopoly groups used the machinery of the state, including navies, armies, and administrative staff, to achieve their ends. And in the course of doing this, they have provided us with yet another example of the identity of purpose uniting ruling classes with the state.

When Lenin wrote his book *Imperialism: The Highest Stage of Capitalism* at the height of World War I, even self-described socialists in Europe criticized him for insisting that the war was one of imperialist plunder. Far from being the "war to end all wars" as many politicians proclaimed, Lenin saw it as just one of the bloodier conflicts into which monopoly capitalism was driving humanity. Lenin's view, which was angrily denounced on all sides during the war, hardly strikes even bourgeois historians as controversial in the final decades of the twentieth century. The slaughter of millions of human beings for the sake of conquering and redividing ever-larger spheres of interest for monopoly capital; the wholesale massacre of civilians; the profitable arms sales; the secret agreements for division of spoils by the victors; the emotional appeals to national honor, freedom, self-determination, and democracy—all of these features of World War I have been features of imperialist wars ever since.

Domination of the global market by monopoly groupings using the state machinery of a handful of "Great Powers" to achieve their goals is the defining characteristic of the *imperialist* stage of capitalism. The leaders of the "Great Powers" typically have described their motives with lofty slogans. However, their actions have spoken louder than their words. One unusually honest foot soldier of monopoly capital, Major General Smedley D. Butler of the United States Marine Corps, summed up his contribution to U.S. foreign policy as follows:

> I spent thirty-three years and four months in active service as a member of our country's most agile military force—the Marine Corps. I served in all commissioned ranks from a second lieutenant to major-general. And during that period I spent most of my time being a high-class muscle man for Big Business, for Wall Street, and for the bankers. In short, I was a racketeer for capitalism. . . .
>
> Thus I helped make Mexico and especially Tampico safe for American oil interests in 1914. I helped make Haiti and Cuba a decent place for the National City Bank boys to collect revenues in. . . . I helped purify Nicaragua for the international banking house of Brown Brothers in 1909–1912. I brought light to the Dominican Republic for American sugar interests in 1916. I helped make Honduras "right" for American fruit companies in 1903. In China in 1927 I helped see to it Standard Oil went its way unmolested. During those years I had, as the boys in the back room would say, a swell racket. I was rewarded with honors, medals, promotion. Looking back on it, I feel I might have given Al Capone a few hints. The best he could do was operate his racket in three city districts. We marines operated on three continents.[3]

Lenin emphasized that the sort of aggression Major General Butler described was not the result of state policies that the "Great Powers" could just as well have refused to adopt. On the contrary, in the era of monopoly capitalism, states that were not in a position to pursue imperialist policies simply did not become "Great Powers" in the first place.

With some exceptions, the era of direct colonial domination has passed. After World War II, colonialism proved to be too difficult to defend in the face of mounting nationalist pressure and rising Marxist influence in Asia, Africa, and Latin America. Moreover, it has become possible to maintain imperialist domination without direct colonial domination. Evidently, monopoly capitalists made a calculation similar to Joseph Kennedy's, and they, like him, concluded that it would be better to give a few "middlemen" in the colonized territories "a piece" rather than to risk losing the "whole pie." By the early 1960s the old colonial powers had lost most of their colonies in Asia, Africa, and elsewhere. One after another, the colonies officially became independent states, some after valiant and terribly costly armed struggles, others after a more or less peaceful changing of the guard.

Although new flags were run up flagpoles with great fanfare, the end of direct colonial domination did not result in a real improvement in the lives of most people in the officially independent states emerging from colonial domination. Many of the new regimes were little more than tools of what has come to be known as *neocolonialism*. Neocolonialism is the indirect exploitation of ex-colonized peoples by means of entirely unbalanced trade relations, the export of capital on terms unfavorable to those on the receiving end, manipulation of the terms of trade, and "development aid." What makes neocolonialism an indirect form of imperialist control is that the local managers for the imperialist powers—the highest ranking political leaders and administrators as well as the army and police personnel—are usually members of the very groups of people they help to keep under foreign economic and political domination.

In spite of the fact that foreign control is indirect, however, imperialist domination and exploitation has become more efficient in the postcolonial era. As early as 1965, Ghanaian leader Kwame Nkrumah summed up the new reality of neocolonialism as follows: "For those who practice it, it means power without responsibility, and for those who suffer from it, it means exploitation without redress."[4]

Even leaders of newly independent states who have sincerely wanted to build independent economies have found themselves in tight binds. Since the poorest states of Asia, Africa, and Latin America do not generate enough savings to finance their own capital formation, they have been unable to compete economically with the ex-colonial powers that were responsible in large part for "underdeveloping" them. Therefore, they must acquire the needed capital from abroad by obtaining foreign investments or loans. To attract foreign investors, however, the leaders of these states must promote the construction of roads, telephone systems, power plants, technical schools, and other infrastructural facilities foreign investors require to make acceptably high profits. New leaders might also have to offer tax breaks, insurance protection, guarantees of profits, and other guarantees, to reduce risks to prospective foreign investors and "sweeten the deals."

It is easy to see, then, that creating a favorable climate for foreign investment requires obtaining large amounts of exported capital in the form of loans. In view of this reality, it is not surprising that even leaders in Asia, Africa, and Latin America who sincerely would have preferred to follow a more independent path have been forced into the familiar pattern of domination by the International Monetary Fund (IMF), the World Bank, and other agencies representing the interests of imperialist states and finance capital.

Peoples under neo-colonial domination are caught in a trap of ever deeper national debt. Imperialist lending institutions and states siphon off most of the economic surplus produced in the societies they dominate, which then must seek further aid and credits from the imperialist states. As a result, states under neo-colonial domination need more exports to service their larger debts. As more value is transferred through this kind of export policy, however, less surplus product remains, and there is consequently a greater need for loans to subsidize state expenditures. By 1990 Africa's debt alone was 272 billion dollars—two and one half times greater than Africa's debt in 1980. For sub-Sahahran Africa, the debt was 174 billion dollars in 1990, as compared to 56 billion dollars in 1980, and its ratio of debt to gross national product was a staggering 112 percent. Debt servicing takes over 30 percent of Africa's total export earnings, and countries on that continent have been sending 4 percent of their gross domestic product to the wealthiest capitalist states, as interest on its debts alone. Thus, what are misleadingly called "developing countries" find themselves locked in a downward spiral of greater exploitation, indebtedness, and poverty.

If we recall the discussion in Chapter 3, it should be clear that lower standards of living mean cheaper labor-power and lower prices for raw materials and other commodities. As long as imports from imperialist-dominated regions continue to fetch low prices, these products of highly exploited labor help to keep profits in the advanced capitalist societies from falling. This, in large part, is what has been behind the prosperity of the advanced capitalist societies, their political stability, and the relatively high standard of living enjoyed by many workers in these societies.

We've seen that the burden of economic crisis in the advanced capitalist societies has been displaced onto workers and peasants in Asia, Africa, Latin America, and elsewhere. In fact, if we recall that many workers in imperialist countries receive dividends from corporate stock and other investments, it could be argued that these profits make it possible for some workers to become partial capitalists themselves. Lenin called the section of a working class that has received the "crumbs" of imperialist superprofits the *aristocracy of labor*. Imperialist superprofits and the existence of an aristocracy of labor help to account for the fact that a minority of monopoly capitalists have been able to maintain overwhelming political and ideological hegemony in the richest capitalist societies for decades.

Despite the well-financed propaganda about the benefits to everyone of "free trade," the gap between rich countries and poor ones has grown. In 1890, for example, Europe was twice as wealthy per capita as China or India. By 1940, it was forty times richer; in 1990, it was seventy times richer. Each year since 1986, at least 43 billion dollars more has flowed from the "South" (that is, the poorer regions of Asia, Africa, Latin America, and elsewhere) to the "North" (that is, the wealthiest countries of Europe, North America, Japan, and elsewhere) than vice versa. Together, states in Latin America, Africa, and Asia pay about three times more every year just to service their foreign debts than the total they receive in development assistance through all channels. These debt payments are, in essence, a forced contribution by the poorest people of the poorest societies to the richest people of the richest societies.

Recognizing this, it should not have come as a surprise when a U.N. study released in 1992 reported that the global gap between rich and poor has doubled since 1960. Fully half the population of Asia, Africa, and Latin America does not have safe drinking water. In these regions, nearly 1 billion people cannot read or write; every night, billions of people go to bed hungry; and 700 million people, mostly women and children, suffer from malnutrition. After hopeful signs in the 1980s, the World Health Organization (WHO) now reports that in those regions smallpox, HIV, tuberculosis, cancer, heart disease, malaria, and other diseases connected with poverty are on the rise again. According to WHO, 14 million children under five years of age die every year from diarrhea and other easily preventable diseases.

To make prospects for the future even more desperate, a brain drain is in full swing throughout the South, as highly skilled and educated people migrate to the North. A United Nations report estimated that in 1989 there were eighty-one scientists and technicians per thousand people in the richest countries of the North, as opposed to nine per thousand in the South. Africa has lost one-third of its skilled workers to European immigration. In Ghana, for example, 60 percent of the doctors trained in the early 1980s now work abroad. The result is an increasing dependency of the South on the North and an even deeper downward spiral of poverty.

A society that is economically dependent is also politically dependent. We can illustrate this point by taking a quick look at the World Bank, with its 170 or so member states. According to Martin Kore, a representative from the Philippines to an international conference on the IMF, the World Bank is

> continuing the patterns that were developed during the colonial period ... and even though our countries in the "South" have gained political

independence, that independence to a large degree is empty because economically speaking, we are even more dependent on the ex-colonial countries than we ever were and the World Bank and the IMF are playing the role of ex-colonial masters.[5]

This sort of domination is now being extended to post–Cold War eastern Europe and what used to be the Soviet Union.

Fidel Castro has argued that the poorest countries should organize themselves into a cartel to collectively renegotiate their debts from a position of strength. It is not surprising that lender banks have threatened countries with financial boycott if they attempt to take Castro's advice.

Imperialism Versus Peace and the Environment

We have seen that by raising the standard of living for a portion of the working class in the advanced capitalist societies, imperialists have secured a measure of political stability at home. This in turn has breathed new life into capitalism internationally.

Another way in which the life of capitalism has been extended has been associated with the name of English economist John Maynard Keynes. To put it briefly, Keynes urged the leaders of capitalist states to undertake programs of public spending in order to maintain the purchasing power of consumers during periods of recession. According to Keynes, states must release money for the construction of roads, bridges, hospitals, and so on, so that unemployed workers from closed factories may be employed in public works and thereby regain their purchasing power. This in turn is supposed to revive effective demand for commodities, thereby spurring production and reactivating idle industrial capacity.[6]

Early in the twentieth century, Rosa Luxemburg drew attention to the part played by the piling up of armaments, generally financed by taxes, as an additional means of capital accumulation. Years later, during the Great Depression of the 1930s, some industrialized capitalist states, following Keynes's advice, developed enormous military programs, which employed millions of workers. Even after World War II, the United States continued to maintain something like a war economy over the course of decades in which it was not officially at war. As a result, the weapons industries on the one hand and state policymakers and high-ranking military personnel on the other merged to form what former U.S. President Eisenhower referred to as the military-industrial complex. The companies that make up part of the military-industrial complex produce large numbers of guns, airplanes, tanks, warships, uniforms, and thousands and thousands of other items for the U.S. military and for export to U.S. allies. In return, their largest stockholders pocket billions and billions of dollars—much of it tax revenue from working-class families. In this way, state military spending and other state "social spending" has come to be yet one more way for big capitalists to appropriate a greater share of surplus value.

In order to justify public funding of the military-industrial complex, politicians, journalists, and professors exaggerated the threat posed by the Soviet Union and other foreign powers. As none other than General Douglas MacArthur, at the end of the McCarthy era, noted:

> Our government has kept us in a perpetual state of fear—kept us in a continual stampede of patriotic fervor—with the cry of a grave national emergency. Always there has been some terrible evil at home or some monstrous foreign power that was going to gobble us up if we did not blindly rally behind it by furnishing the exhorbitant funds demanded. Yet, in retrospect, these disasters seem never to have happened, seem never to have been quite real.[7]

U.S. leaders have periodically invented illusory "national security threats"—in Korea, Vietnam, Cuba, Nicaragua, and lots of other places including the tiny island of Grenada!—to justify expanding their military-industrial complex. Nowhere is this clearer than in the Middle East, where for decades the United States has used its zionist base in Palestine not only to ensure western control of the region's oil reserves and the Suez Canal but also to further militarize the region, turning it into a dumping ground for expensive military hardware.

MacArthur's words have never rung truer than today, in the wake of the collapse of what Ronald Reagan dubbed the "Evil Empire." Years after the disappearance of the "Soviet threat" the United States continues to spend hundreds of billions of dollars annually on armaments including twelve aircraft carrier fighting groups, a new generation of fighter bombers, thousands of active nuclear weapons, and a program to militarize outer space.

The fact that imperialist states continue to deploy so many weapons of mass destruction indicates that they are still prepared to risk not only the lives of the present generation but also the very ability of generations yet unborn to inhabit a large part of our planet. This shows as well as anything else that when the environment comes into conflict with the perceived interests of monopoly capital, capital comes first.

Over one hundred years ago, Marx and Engels identified the exploitation of workers by capitalists with waste of natural resources and degradation of the environment. In the first volume of *Capital*, for example, Marx wrote:

> The more a country starts its development on the foundation of modern industry, like the United States, for example, the more rapid is the process of destruction. Capitalistic production, therefore, develops technology, and the combining together of various processes into a social whole, only by sapping the original sources of all wealth—the soil and the labourer.[8]

This observation has never been more appropriate than in the present period of imperialism, when rulers in the South, forced to service their debts to international lending institutions, permit projects that have caused enormous damage and waste of the earth's natural resources. International lending institutions, western corporations, and local capitalists are responsible for the ongoing destruction of rain forests in the Amazon Basin and elsewhere. Huge areas of the western part of Africa have been turned into toxic waste dumps for western corporations. Topsoil throughout Africa has been exhausted and eroded, and vast areas of sub-Saharan Africa have been turned into desert land, thanks in large part to the policies of imperialist states and lending institutions.

World Bank vice president Lawrence Summers provided an insight into their policy calculations when, in a candid moment, he wrote:

> Health impairing pollution should be done in the country with the lowest cost, which will be the country with the lowest wages.... I think the economic logic behind dumping a load of toxic waste in the lowest-wage country is impeccable and we should face up to that.... I've always thought that underpopulated countries in Africa are vastly underpolluted, their air quality is probably vastly inefficiently high compared to Los Angeles or Mexico City.... Concern over an agent that causes one in a million chance of prostate cancer is obviously going to be much higher in a country where people survive to get prostate cancer than in a country where under-five mortality is 200 per thousand.[9]

Tragically, however, self-described Marxists are also responsible for destroying and wasting natural resources. Leaders of the former Soviet Union and other supposedly socialist countries pushed centralized heavy industrial production on a large scale while for the most part ignoring the impact of this policy on the environment. This resulted in the destruction of the Aral Sea in Central Asia, terrible air and water pollution in eastern Europe and elsewhere, exhaustion of topsoil in Central Asia, the construction of unsafe nuclear power plants, extremely inefficient use of generated power, and other environmental disasters.

And this in turn had a predictable impact on the humans who inhabited these areas. Environmental pollution accounts in large part for the fact that life expectancy fell during the last decades of the Soviet Union. According to one study, for example, the number of cancer patients per 10,000 inhabitants of the Soviet city of Yerevan quadrupled between 1965 and 1985. The same study went on to report that in a fifteen-year period the number of mentally retarded children increased fourfold, cases of anemia increased fivefold, and the number of premature births increased sevenfold. Similar increases were reported for congenital birth defects, infant morbidity, and pneumonia. Environmental pollution almost certainly was a major cause of the deteriorating health conditions in Yerevan and throughout the Soviet Union.

The experience of the former Soviet Union and other self-described socialist countries stands as a terribly costly lesson for Marxists today. Marxists, of course, are dedicated to improving the lives of the underfed, underclothed, and poorly housed majority; nevertheless, Marxists can—and for the sake of future generations, they *should*—seek solutions that do not endanger the environment and waste resources.

Marxists have much to learn from environmentalists. By the same token, however, environmentalists have much to learn from Marxists. Billion-dollar advertising industries promote waste and greedy consumerism; popular demands for energy-efficent mass-transit systems have regularly been derailed by automobile corporations and oil companies; the IMF and the World Bank appear to have dedicated themselves to transforming large areas of the South into strip mines and toxic waste dumps, and poverty, enforced ignorance, and the oppression of women are responsible in large part for current levels of population growth. If environmentalists are to attack the root causes of the worst pollution and waste, then they will need to gain a broader, historical materialist perspective, a perspective that connects environmental protection issues with the problems of super-exploitation and indebtedness in the South and hence to imperialist domination.

Imperialism

We will return to the urgent issue of protecting our environment in the next and final chapter. Before going on, however, it might help to sum up what has been said in this chapter and to draw a couple of conclusions.

As we have seen, economic production in capitalist countries has been increasingly collectivized. The task of managing the largest firms and corporations has been taken out of the hands of the owners and put into the hands of professional managers employed by the owners; big business and the state have merged ever more closely, and an interdependent global division of labor has largely replaced isolated small-scale production.

In these and other ways, capitalism has already solved many of the problems that have until recently made it impossible to transfer the means of production from a few private hands into the possession of those who are directly involved in economic production.

At the same time, however, the more productive labor has become under capitalism, the more surplus product capitalists have been able to appropriate. Therefore, the state (which, as we have seen, has come to merge ever more closely with monopoly capital), opposes any fundamental challenge to capitalist ownership of the means of production. Because of this, communism cannot develop within capitalist society the way capitalism developed within feudal societies in medieval Europe.

In order to achieve workers' power in the era of imperialism, then, it will almost certainly be necessary to defeat the organized violence of the state. This is why Marxists put so much emphasis on the need to build the sort of working-class organizations that will one day be capable of fighting and defeating the armed might of monopoly capitalist state power. And this is also why workers today need historical materialism as a guide to political action. Only in this way can they gain an accurate view of what Marx called the "line of march" leading to socialism.

Summary

Key terms discussed in this chapter include *concentration of production, monopoly capitalism, finance capital, imperialism, neocolonialism,* and *aristocracy of labor.*

Since the last quarter of the nineteenth century, capitalist competition has lead to the concentration of production in fewer and fewer hands. Monopolies have become increasingly important to economic life in capitalist societies.

Banks and the credit system also contributed greatly to the concentration of production and capital. The big banks have merged with industry and have come to dominate it, resulting in the formation of finance capital.

The export of capital has surpassed the export of commodities in importance. Today, the international circulation of capital in a number of forms (including state loans) is extremely important.

At the beginning of the imperialist era, a few powerful capitalist states competed with each other to carve out spheres of interest, which they dominated directly as colonies. Later, after these colonies achieved a measure of political independence, imperialist domination took the less direct but more efficient form of neocolonialism. Today, institutions such as the International Monetary Fund and the World Bank play a crucial role in maintaining imperialist domination of the globe.

Meanwhile, the gap between rich and poor gapes ever wider. In the richest capitalist societies, the most highly skilled workers form an aristocracy of labor, which benefits somewhat from imperialist superprofits. At the same time, imperialism has lead to increased national oppression, the spread of weapons of mass destruction, massive poverty, starvation, and environmental pollution. Today, at the threshhold of a new century, we face the same stark choice that Rosa Luxemburg recognized at the beginning of the twentieth century: socialism or barbarism.

A Note on Further Readings

Ever since he wrote *Imperialism: The Highest Stage of Capitalism* (New York: International Publishers, 1969) at the height of World War I, Lenin's analysis of monopoly capitalism has been confirmed over and over again. Although the face of global capitalism has changed greatly since 1916, this book remains required reading for students of the international scene today.

More recent introductory texts on the subject of imperialism include: Paul Baran's *The Political Economy of Growth* (New York: Monthly Review Press, 1957); Jack Woddis's *An Introduction to Neo-Colonialism* (New York: International Publishers, 1967—but unfortunately not readily available in print); Pierre Jalee's *The Pillage of the Third World* (New York: Monthly Review Press, 1968); Harry Magdoff's *Imperialism: From the Colonial Age to the Present* (New York: Monthly Review Press, 1979); and Berch Berberoghlu's

The Internationalization of Capital: Imperialism and Capitalist Development on a World Scale (New York: Praeger, 1987). Cheryl Payer's *Lent and Lost: Foreign Credit and Third World Development* (London: Zed Press, 1991) provides a more up-to-date view into the workings of international lending institutions.

Today, Japan and the European Economic Community rival the United States as economic powers, although the United States is both the sole undisputed military superpower and the largest debtor of any nation. Meanwhile, many political leaders in the South, whether democratically elected or not, have become little more than local managers for the IMF and the World Bank, within a global system of intensified imperialist domination. On the threshhold of a new century, Marxists face the enormous challenge of coming to grips with these new realities, both intellectually and politically.

Walter Rodney (1942–1980)

Marxists of Africa

During the 1980s some 12 million people on the continent of Africa died as a result of famine and war caused in large part by state policies, agencies, and lending institutions of the capitalist West. This catastrophe was only one more chapter in a five hundred-year history of monstrous abuse and exploitation on the African continent. Sadly, precious little has improved for most Africans since the end of direct colonial rule in much of Africa during the 1950s and 1960s. Foreign rulers have been replaced by equally brutal and greedy African despots obedient only to imperialist agencies, foreign corporations, and international lending institutions.

For decades, some of the best daughters and sons of Africa have fought for a brighter future for the impoverished people of their rich continent. Among the thousands of revolutionaries whose names deserve to be mentioned are: South African Communist Party leaders Albert Nzula and Moses Kotane; Dr. Felix Moumie, leader of the People's Union of Cameroon, or PUC (murdered by French terrorists in 1960); Patrice Lumumba, founder and leader of the Congolese National Movement (murdered by agents of the CIA in 1961); Ernest Ouande, another outstanding leader of the PUC (executed in 1970); Moroccan revolutionary Ben Barka (kidnapped in 1965 and killed); Abdullah Kassim Hanga, vice president of the Afro-Shirazi Party in

Zanzibar (executed without trial in 1970); Ahmed Maghoub and Joseph Garang, leaders and theoreticians of the Communist Party of Sudan (both executed by the dictator Numeiri in 1971, along with the entire Central Committee of the party); Amilcar Cabral, theoretician and leader of the African Party for the Independence of Guinea and Cape Verde (assassinated in 1973); Eduardo Mondlane, founder of the FRELIMO party in Mozambique (assassinated in 1969); Marcelino Dos Santos, vice president of FRELIMO; Agostinho Neto, poet, revolutionary and first president of Angola; Samora Machel, first president of Mozambique (who died in 1986 when his airplane went down near the border of the racist Republic of South Africa); and Chris Hani, general secretary of the South African Communist Party (assassinated by a terrorist on April 10, 1993).

These African Marxists—and tens of thousands of other courageous men and women—devoted everything they had to the struggle against colonial armies, CIA-backed tyrants, and the local "authentically African" security chiefs of the IMF. The example of their lives will inspire a new generation of African Marxists in the twenty-first century.

* * *

The book *How Europe Underdeveloped Africa* (most recently published by Howard University Press in 1982) is a clearly written and powerful account of the colonial domination of Africa, from the 1400s to the late 1950s. The author of the book, Guyanese historian Walter Rodney, was assassinated in 1980, suffering the same fate as so many of his comrades on the African continent.

Notes

1. Refer to the Introduction.

2. It should be pointed out, however, that export of capital from imperialist countries to neo-colonies is no longer as crucial for imperialism as it was in the early part of the twentieth century.

3. Quoted in: Richard O. Boyer and Herbert M. Morais, *Labor's Untold Story* (New York: United Electrical, Radio and Machine Workers of America, 1955), p. 241.

4. Kwame Nkrumah, *Neo-Colonialism: The Last Stage of Imperialism* (New York: International Publishers, 1965), p. xi.

5. "People's Forum on the World Bank and the IMF," Bangkok, Thailand (Oct. 7–17, 1991).

6. Governments that have followed Keynes's advice, however, have not been able to remove a serious and stubborn flaw in the capitalist mode of production: the tendency of the productive forces to expand indefinitely, while at the same time effective demand undergoes only limited growth.

7. Address to stockholders of Sperry Rand Corporation, 1957. Quoted in Felix Green's *The Enemy: Notes on Imperialism and Revolution* (London: Jonathan Cape, 1970), p. 203.

8. Karl Marx, *Capital* Vol. 1 (New York: International Publishers, 1967), pp. 506–507.

9. World Bank internal memo dated December 12, 1991, and subsequently leaked to the public. Quoted in *Race and Class* Vol. 34 (July–September 1992), p. 85.

6

What Do Marxists Fight For?

We do not claim that Marx knew or Marxists knew the road to socialism down to the last detail. It would be nonsense to claim anything of the kind. What we know is the direction of the road, and the class forces that follow it; the specific, practical details will come to light only through the experience of the millions when they take things into their own hands.

—*V.I. Lenin*

At the beginning of this primer I suggested that what collapsed in eastern Europe in the late 1980s was a far cry from socialism, let alone communism. But what are socialism and communism, and what is the relationship between them? These are important questions for Marxists because they are questions about their medium- and long-term goals. These questions will be considered in the remaining pages.

First let's clear up a common confusion about words. Marxists have not always used the words *socialism* and *communism* consistently. Sometimes Marxists have referred to communism as "the highest form of socialism." At other times they have referred to socialism as "the first, immature phase of communism," and to communism as "the higher phase of communist society." Other Marxists have spoken of socialism as a classless society of the future and the most distant goal for which workers should fight.

The confusion is entirely avoidable, however, as long as we keep in mind that the founders of historical materialism usually referred to socialism and communism in the following ways:

Communism is a possible mode of production in which labor is highly productive, but there is no private appropriation of the surplus product of society, hence no exploitation. Production is for social use, not for the market. A communist society is a society in which the

113

communist mode of production is dominant, hence there is no class conflict or state repression.

Socialism, by contrast, is the period of transition from capitalism to communism. A socialist society is one characterized by the state rule of workers as a class over capitalists.

I will discuss these definitions in a bit more depth, but first we should notice that socialism and communism are basically different sorts of things: Communism is a possible mode of production, whereas socialism is a historical transition period[1] between the capitalist present and the communist future. A socialist society, then, is a society going through such a transition, whereas a communist society would be one in which the communist mode of production is dominant. What socialism has in common with what is sometimes called "full" communism is an absence of massive exploitation through wage labor and the control of the productive process by the direct producers themselves. Nevertheless, as we will see, the two sorts of societies are very different.

Keeping this in mind, it is surely misleading to describe the fall of the self-described "socialist" regimes of eastern Europe as the "collapse of communism." After all, it would be silly to claim that a building has collapsed when that building does not yet exist. And this is especially true in the case of communism, which as we shall see does not yet exist even in the form of a blueprint, but only as a rough sketch. Indeed, if socialism is workers' power, as Marxists define it to be, then what took place in eastern Europe was not even the "collapse of socialism," let alone of communism. This point should become even clearer by the end of this chapter.

Socialism

When Marx was only twenty-five years old, he wrote that "if the designing of the future and the proclamation of ready-made solutions for all time is not our affair, then we realize all the more clearly what we have to accomplish in the present—I am speaking of a *ruthless criticism of everything existing.*"[2] Among the targets of Marx's "ruthless criticism" were the utopian socialists who drew up detailed plans for future societies without carefully or realistically answering the question: How is such a society supposed to come into existence? Utopian socialists such as the Frenchmen Charles Fourier and Claude Henri de Saint Simone, or the English industrialist Robert Owen imagined societies that were supposed to be more just or ethical than existing societies. These and other utopian socialists worked hard to try to realize their visions. Owen even founded his own experimental communities in the United States and elsewhere. Nevertheless, the utopian socialists failed to realize their visions.

The founders of historical materialism, by contrast, wrote very little on the subject of socialism and even less about communism. What's more, most of what they did write on these subjects was in the form of heated arguments against what they felt were flights of fancy about a future social order. This was the case, for example, in Marx's *Critique of the Gotha Program,* Engels's *Anti-Duhring,* and Lenin's *The State and Revolution.*

If Marx, Engels, and Lenin wrote about the postcapitalist future infrequently—and then only with caution—it is clear, nonetheless, that they recognized common ownership of the means of production and economic planning as basic features of both socialism and communism. Public ownership of the means of production and a planned economy may be characteristics of socialism; nevertheless, it would be a mistake to conclude, as some Soviet writers did, that these are jointly sufficient conditions of socialism (let alone communism!)—at least as Marx, Engels, Lenin, Luxemburg, and Gramsci conceived of socialism. In *Anti-Duhring,* for example, Engels made it clear that state ownership of the means of production alone "is not the solution of the conflict"[3] between socialized production and private ownership. As long as widespread extraction of surplus value through wage labor takes place, state (or "public") ownership of the means of production could amount to state capitalism, rather than socialism.

Furthermore, there is no reason why this sort of state ownership cannot be combined with planning. In fact, advanced capitalist societies such as the United States do indeed have largely planned economies with a great deal of intervention by the state in such areas as monetary policy, tax policy, and state spending on social programs and the military. Indeed, as we saw in Chapter 5, capitalist economic planning today extends far beyond the borders of individual states.

The founders of historical materialism did not define socialism as state planning plus social ownership of the means of production. Rather, they conceived of it as first and foremost the self-emancipation of the working class: For them, Socialism is workers' power. More strictly speaking, assuming a relatively high level of development of the productive forces and the productivity of labor, socialism is a state of affairs in which the economically productive majority of society is the ruling class, rather than the minority that owns means of production.

There are many misperceptions about how goods are to be distributed in a socialist society. We should mention at least two points, to correct the most common misperceptions.

First, Marxists don't believe that everyone should receive the same payment or basket of goods, regardless of how long and how hard they work or how highly skilled they are. Under socialism, distribution of means of consumption will take place according to the single standard "to each according to labor contributed." The only exceptions to this standard would be assistance to orphans, the aged, people with disabilities, and others incapable of supporting themselves. Under capitalism, by contrast, this standard does not apply to most of the richest capitalists, who originally inherited their wealth and will never have to perform productive work their entire lives.

Let's take a slightly closer look at the standard "to each according to labor contributed." In a socialist society, a carpenter who works thirty hours a week and produces ten chairs in that time will receive more than a carpenter who works twenty hours a week and produces six chairs. Moreover, a worker who has spent four extra years in school learning a specialized skill will be paid more than a less skilled worker. If, for example, it takes twice as long to train an engineer as to train a carpenter, the engineer's salary might be twice as great. Additional incentives might also be necessary to encourage initiative and efficiency. Thus, socialism is likely for a long time to sanction differences in household incomes in the form of unequal distribution of consumer goods and services. Recognizing this, Lenin wrote that:

> The first phase of communism therefore, still cannot produce justice and equality; differences, and unjust differences, in wealth will still exist, but the exploitation of man by man will have become impossible, because it will be impossible to seize as private property the means of production, the factories, machines, land, and so on.[4]

Notice that Lenin was referring to a notion of justice exemplified by the communist motto: "From each according to ability, to each according to need." It is important to note, however, that even according to this notion of justice, resources will not be shared out equally to each worker: A household with six members might well receive more than a household with two members, because the larger household is likely to require more means of consumption to sustain the same standard of living.

Second, it is not true that under socialism—or even communism—everyone will receive the full value of their labor. "To each according to labor contributed" does not mean "What you have made by your own labor, that you will receive." Indeed, the latter slogan would spell disaster for socialism, even if we qualify it by recognizing the social obligation to support the young, the aged, and those incapable of supporting themselves. If every worker were to receive the full product of their labor, there would be no possiblity of expanding and improving production. It would not be possible to invest in upgraded equipment, to add more work stations, or to improve transport systems. Under socialism, then, as under capitalism, the state would have to appropriate part of the surplus product to improve production. Unlike capitalism, however, the surplus appropriated by a socialist state would benefit workers first and foremost, making it possible to invest, for example, in upgraded infrastructure to reduce the length of the workday.

True, under socialism workers would receive a greater basket of goods than they currently do under capitalism. This is because with the collective ownership of means of production there would be no private profit to diminish returns to direct producers. Nevertheless, carpenters who produce ten chairs a week still would not be able to trade their weekly basket of goods for ten chairs. In other words, products would be distributed in proportion to the work done, but this proportion would be less than one to one.

As we saw in Chapter 2, each mode of production has its own unique relations of production. Under capitalism, these relations of production are characterized by wage labor and private ownership of the means of production. Under communism, by contrast, relations of production are characterized by production for social use and social ownership of the means of production. It is important to notice, however, that there are no relations of production unique to the period of transition from capitalism to communism. Depending on the society in question—the level of development of its productive forces, its degree of integration into the global division of labor, and the amount of economic development that has taken place since workers gained state power—there may be a combination of production for the market, together with some degree of production for use, or perhaps even small- and medium-scale private appropriation of part of the surplus product.

This last observation has a consequence that deserves to be emphasized: Because socialism is not capable of sustaining its own characteristic social relations, it is misleading to think of socialism as a mode of production. Rather, as we have already found out, it is a transitional phase between two sorts of societies dominated by two different modes of production—capitalist and communist.

Since socialism does not "automatically" generate its own social relations as does capitalism, social relations under socialism would have to be sustained by early education, moral pressure, and other conscious, noneconomic processes. From this we can see why state intervention and planning as well as public education and "culture" would have an important role to play in a socialist society. This task is likely to be made more difficult still because class conflict—between small proprietors and workers, for example, or between socialist and imperialist states—would probably survive for a long time after socialist revolution.

These observations underscore the view that there is no magic formula for building socialism, no model to be copied in each and every case. To attempt to come up with a magic formula would amount to what Marx described as "writing recipes for the cook shops of the future." Nevertheless, we can at least make a few cautious generalizations.

For one thing, the major means of production would be nationalized in the wake of socialist revolution. This would include the major industrial and agricultural enterprises, land, transportation, communication, banks, and credit institutions. Perhaps for a long time state economic planners would have to take the market into account as a means of making consumer prices conform to costs of production, and incentives could be offered for innovation and hard work. As we already learned, it might even be the case that exploitation on a stictly limited scale (in the form of small-scale capitalist enterprises) would have to be tolerated.

In any case, we would not expect capitalism to disappear immediately after a socialist revolution. Once they were to defeat capitalist rulers and gain political power, the goal of workers should be to aim as rapidly as possible at eliminating unemployment and overproduction. In the more highly industrialized societies, the biggest gaps in wealth and income could rapidly be reduced through tax policy (higher corporate taxes, steeply graduated income taxes, capital gains, inheritance taxes, and so on) and other forms of legislation. Speaking more broadly, under socialism the system of production for private profit, although it might perhaps not entirely disappear, would be dramatically curtailed.

There can be no workers' power without workers managing their own factories, farms, workshops, and offices. Workers' self-management could take place at several levels: at the "micro-level" of the firm; at the industrial branch level, and—as far as is technologically possible—at the "national" level, or the level of society as a whole. Workers themselves may judge that special administrative staff and managers who are not workers may still be necessary on a case-by-case basis. But this sort of bureaucracy should be kept to a bare minimum, to avoid the dangers of abuse of power against which Luxemburg and Lenin warned so often. At the national level, key decisions about the divison of the national product, priorities for using scarce resources, options and priorities for the use of the social surplus and tax revenues, and so on, would be discussed openly, and alternatives presented.

In order to make this sort of direct participation and discussion possible, it would be necessary to cut the workweek, at least in the most highly industrialized countries. This would allow workers adequate time to discuss and manage their own affairs. Extending education into adulthood and breaking the corporate monopoly on the means of communication would also help the majority of the voting population to make informed choices.

Machine production, computers, robotics, and a wide range of other innovations have made it technically possible to transform the division of labor as it exists in capitalist societies today, by reducing the need for the heaviest sorts of manual labor and drudgery. Unfortunately, when labor-saving technologies are introduced into capitalist workplaces, workers typically lose their jobs. Under socialism, by contrast, labor-saving technologies could be adopted on a larger scale, to shorten the working day, rather than to increase profits for capitalists. As a result, the division of labor between "brain-work" and manual labor could be greatly diminished.

Nevertheless, just because the division of labor might diminish in some fields of production, this does not warrant the conclusion that the increasingly complex tasks of "administrating things" would necessarily one day be simplified to such an extent that, as Lenin had hoped, any cook could accomplish them. It appears that Marx, Engels, and Lenin were too ready to adopt this idea from one or another nineteenth-century utopian socialist. As a result, they probably exaggerated the degree to which the division of labor could be "abolished," while still maintaining the high level of productivity of labor necessary to sustain a communist society. Gramsci, among other Marxists, criticized this notion.

If the number of socialist societies were to increase along with the productivity of labor, and if the remaining capitalist states were no longer to pose a threat to the existence of socialism, a socialist commonwealth might then become a global reality. And this in turn would set the stage for what in the last section of this chapter we will call "the withering away of the state."

Learning from Defeats

Marxists have made many tragic mistakes in the twentieth century. Some of these mistakes have been accompanied by deep theoretical failures. In this section we'll consider three such mistakes, having to do with women's rights, environmentalism, and democracy.

Women's Rights

After gaining some immediate and important benefits from the Bolshevik Revolution, women in the Soviet Union suffered one setback after another in the following decades. Few women ever achieved positions of influence in the state, and, as time passed, many women were expected to shoulder housework as well as low-paying jobs. In spite of this dismal record, however, Mikhail Gorbachev, then General Secretary of the Communist Party of the Soviet Union, openly advocated sending women even further back to their "maternal roles" in the household!

The relationship between the oppression of women and class exploitation is currently a subject of much valuable debate. Whatever the outcome of these debates, however, one thing is clear: The Soviet record regarding women's rights made a mockery of Marxism.

Gorbachev's view compares very unfavorably to the views of the founders of historical materialism. In *The Origin of the Family, Private Property and the State,* for example, Engels argued that the first class oppression "coincides with that of the female sex by the male."[5] This oppression, he said, resulted from the victory of private property over primitive communal property. Accordingly, those who recognize that private ownership of the means of production is not an eternal and natural state of affairs should also stand opposed to the notion that women are naturally inferior to men.

Recognizing this, most if not all Marxists also emphasize that, for better or for worse, the family is a changing institution. In *The Teachings of Karl Marx,* Lenin wrote:

> A new kind of family life, changes in the position of women and in the upbringing of the younger generation, are being prepared by the highest forms of modern capitalism; the labour of women and children, the break-up of the patriarchal family by capitalism, necessarily assume in contemporary society the most terrible, disastrous, and repulsive forms.[6]

In the last quarter of the twentieth century, Lenin's observations have come back to haunt us. The patriarchal family headed by the father who is the sole breadwinner is an exception to the rule in several highly industrialized capitalist countries such as the United States, with its 50 percent divorce rate, its "feminization of poverty," and so on. Nevertheless, Lenin continued, quoting from the first volume of *Capital:* "Large-scale industry, by assigning to women and to young persons of both sexes a decisive role in the socially organized process of production, and a role which has to be fulfilled outside the home, is building the new economic foundation for a higher form of the family and of the relations between the sexes."[7]

Rosa Luxemburg believed that women can achieve their full liberation only with the triumph of socialist revolution and the elimination of women's economic bondage to the bourgeois family. Although there is no good reason to believe that socialism itself would automatically bring with it an end to male domination of women, one thing appears likely: socialism is a necessary precondition for destroying the worst and most widespread forms of oppression of women. Furthermore, judging from past experience, any future advances some women may make under capitalism are likely to be half-measures that are always in danger of being reversed.

Environmentalism

To avoid repeating errors that in the past have served Marxists so poorly, Marxists should put less stress on centralized heavy industrial production. Marxists could draw lessons from the fact that, although the concentration of capital continues at a rapid pace, many branches of production in the most advanced capitalist countries today (including information systems, communications, and electronics) have come to be decentralized, medium-scale industries. Furthermore, even Marxists in the most highly industrialized societies might have a lot to learn from such sources as the women of the Chipko environmentalist movement in northern India, the small-scale rubber tappers and nut harvesters in Brazil's Amazon Basin, or the people participating in village-scale natural methane production projects in southern India.

With the defeat of imperialism on a global scale, we should also expect new and very different priorities when it comes to trade relations, extending credit, and funding "development" projects in the less industrialized countries of the South. These priorities would reflect a new reality in which a few wealthy states in the North no longer dictate terms of credit, trade relations, technology transfers, and the international division of labor to the South. Moreover, socialism could set the stage for efficient and voluntary population control, since, judging by the lessons of the past, the most efficient way to curtail population growth without resorting to force is to combine voluntary birth control programs with social programs and campaigns for women's literacy.

Beyond this, however, Marxists need to recognize that the level of consumption in the richest societies of the North simply cannot be sustained within the limits of technological developments in the foreseeable future. These societies, which make up less than one-fourth of the earth's population, consume 80 percent of all the resources consumed by humanity. What's more, the United States alone, with only 5 percent of the earth's population, consumes 35 percent of the total resources consumed and is responsible for 25 percent of the earth's greenhouse gas emissions (mostly carbon dioxide). And when we take into account that a large portion of the U.S. population does not have a high level of consumption, it becomes clear that a very small percentage of the earth's population is wrecklessly consuming a large part of its nonrenewable resources.

Many people, Marxists and non-Marxists alike, believe that this sort of wreckless consumption should be discouraged, even if it requires a drop in the average standard of living in the richest societies. Furthermore, many people recognize a need to fight against the lie promoted by corporate advertising agencies that the more commodities people consume the happier they will be. Consumption is not the magic key to individual happiness, and access to more and more consumer goods is not necessarily the final standard of how well-off a society is.

Democracy

This might be a good place to say a few words about a term that is very easy to misunderstand these days. The term *dictatorship of the proletariat* comes from Marx and Engels's writings on the Paris Commune of 1871 and gained greater currency thanks to Lenin. In *The Class Struggles in France* (1850), Marx described the dictatorship of the proletariat as "the necessary transit point to the abolition of classes generally, to the abolition of all the relations of production on which they rest, to the abolition of all the social relations that correspond to these relations of production, to the revolutionizing of all the ideas that result from these social relations."[8] In *The State and Revolution,* Lenin underscored this view, referring to the dictatorship of the proletariat as a "political transitional period" between capitalism and communism. From these passages, then, it would appear that the dictatorship of the proletariat is workers' power—it is the political state of affairs under socialism.

According to Marx, the purpose of the dictatorship of the proletariat is to "raise the proletariat the position of the ruling class, to win the battle of democracy."[9] This equation of a dictatorship with democracy may sound strange at first, until we realize that Marx, Engels, Luxemburg, and Lenin all contrasted the dictatorship of the proletariat not with *democracy* of the proletariat, but with dictatorship of the *bourgeoisie*. In fact, if by democracy we mean majority rule, then it is deeply democratic to demand that workers and their family members be made the ruling class, rather than the small minority of capitalists who make up the ruling classes of most countries today. This is why Rosa Luxemburg said that the dictatorship of the proletariat makes possible "unlimited democracy."[10]

Many people who don't like the term dictatorship of the proletariat fail to recognize that class dictatorships are already in power in such democracies as the United States, Japan, and Germany. In this sense, then, class rule is always a dictatorship, even when it takes the form of a democratic republic or a parliamentary democracy.

Since Stalin came to power in the Soviet Union, however, the term dictatorship of the proletariat has come to be associated with the dictatorship not of workers but of a Party or even one tyrant. Partly because of this association, one Communist Party after another has abandoned the slogan.

Whatever the fate of the term dictatorship of the proletariat, however, one thing is clear: No capitalist ruling class has ever given up state power without a fight. So if Marxists are ever to achieve their aims, they need to organize themselves in such a way as to confront and defeat the counterrevolutionary violence of the ruling class.

The dictatorship of the proletariat was originally envisioned as taking the form of workers', peasants', and soldiers' councils, or *soviets,* in Russian. The soviets were the main institutional way in which the peoples of Russia excercized political power during the attempted revolution of 1905 and the successful revolution of 1917. Delegates to a regional or city soviet were usually elected by a show of hands in a meeting of workers, peasants, or soldiers in a factory, farm, or military unit, and any delegate could be replaced at any time. Like the Paris Commune, the soviets were both legislative and executive bodies; once a session of the soviet closed, its delegates personally saw to the implementation of policies decided upon.

In the course of events the soviets came to act as a governing authority, making and enforcing laws, settling disputes, and even bringing in an eight-hour workday. This arrangement brought large numbers of workers into close contact with the governing institutions, and it did so with a minimum of what Lenin identified as the young Soviet state's worst internal enemy," the "evil" of bureaucracy.[11]

Unfortunately, the desperate situation immediately after the 1917 Bolshevik Revolution was not conducive to this or any sort of direct democracy. Capitalist governments imposed an economic embargo against the revolutionary state, the armies of a dozen foreign countries invaded Soviet Russia, and the Bolsheviks were forced into a costly civil war at a time when Russia had not yet emerged from the devastation of World War I. By 1922, under these terribly difficult conditions, the soviets had been placed entirely under the central control of the Communist Party. And even more tragically, by the time the foreign invaders had been repelled and the civil war had been won (that is, at the time of Lenin's death in 1924), when the councils could have been changed back into multiparty bodies, they were deliberately transformed into little more than bullhorns for relaying decisions of the party leadership to the masses. Indeed, Stalin referred to the soviets as "levers" or "drive belts" of the Communist Party, not the state.

A variety of postrevolutionary experiences, some successful and many unsuccessful, provide lessons about how to avoid the errors of the past. Evidently, one of the most important measures for institutionalizing democracy within a socialist state is sharply to separate the party structure from that of the state.[12]

Moreover, as Luxemburg noted, a multiparty system of representative democracy is almost always the best basis upon which to build participatory democracy. Recent and not-so-recent events show through negative examples that multiparty democracy actually strengthens a ruling workers' party in the long run, by exposing corruption, sharpening debate, and requiring Communists to prove through deeds, not just words, that theirs is the party that most consistently upholds the demands of the working class.

Many Marxists today are convinced that they need to put greater emphasis on defending the rights of freedom of speech, assembly, press, conscience, travel, and so on, and that they need to build institutions to guarantee that these rights will not be violated by the state. They also recognize that trade unions should be entirely independent of the state, and the right to strike should be guaranteed by the constitution. Indeed, without these freedoms, the Marxist call for the self-emancipation of the working class would amount to little more than a slogan advanced in bad faith. Moreover, Marxists are among those who have traditionally held that these "negative rights" should be supplemented with such "positive rights" as the rights to decent housing, health care, and jobs.

Communism

Marx and Lenin would have scoffed at Stalin's triumphant declaration in the 1950s that the USSR was on the threshhold of building a classless communist society. They understood that political leaders and economic planners cannot short-circuit the transition from one mode of production to another simply by proclamation. And this observation is especially true of poor, largely nonindustrial societies like the old Soviet Union.

When we review what the founders of historical materialism had to say about communism, we find that most of their statements appear in the form of claims about what communism will *not* be like. Consider, for example, Marx's well-known statement in the *Critique of the Gotha Program:*

> In a higher phase of communist society, after the enslaving subordination of the individual to the division of labor, and therewith also the antithesis between mental and physical labor, has vanished; after labor has become not only a means of life but life's prime want; after the productive forces have also increased with the all-round development of the individual, and all the springs of cooperative wealth flow more abundantly—only then can the narrow horizon of bourgeois right be crossed in its entirety and society inscribe on its banners: "from each according to his ability, to each according to his needs!"[13]

This very general statement was aimed against some working-class leaders who Marx felt were "writing recipes for the cook shops of the future." For one thing, Marx recognized that bourgeois right—that is, the habit of thinking that "I have it coming to me because I worked for it"—is far too deeply rooted in capitalist relations of production to be done away with in a generation simply by, say, reeducating young people. In a communist society, humans will be so different that they will take the slogan "to each according to need" for granted, perhaps in the way we today take bourgeois right for granted. In order for humans this different to appear, however, big changes will have to take place over a long period of time, including the appearance of an entirely new set of social relations.

Marx, Engels, and Lenin did not just dream up the most rational, humane, or just scheme for organizing society. For them, as we have seen, the material basis for socialism and a gradual transition to communism is already being laid by capitalism, in the form of widespread industrial production and a socialized labor process, socialized consumption, communications, transportation, and so on. As we saw, workers' power would free the already-socialized productive forces from the fetters imposed upon their development by private ownership of the means of production. If social ownership of the means of production were combined with a high level of productivity of labor, people would not have to work as long to produce what they need. What is more, people would not want to work as long, since the profit motive would have disappeared over time, and there would be no corporate advertising to constantly create new needs in people for gadgets and fashions.

Increasingly, production would be for use, not for the market. Commodity production would be eliminated step-by-step, until all or most of what would be produced would simply be products, not commodities. These products would not be bought and sold; rather, they would simply be distributed to whomever needed them. Furthermore, if commodity production were to be eliminated, there would be no need for money. The socialist motto "To each according to labor contributed" would give way to the communist motto "To each according to need." This would mark the end of bourgeois right and would signal the appearance on the scene of a new type of person, a person who is the ensemble of very different social relations. As a result, individuals would relate to each other and to their environment in ways that perhaps we today cannot imagine.

The basis of both socialist and communist production is social ownership of the means of production and distribution. Under socialism, joint ownership of the means of production by workers would have been established. With the disappearance of class differences, joint ownership of the means of production by everyone in society would become the reality. With the elimination of commodity production economic exploitation would disappear. Without either exploiters or exploited, class antagonisms would disappear, along with classes themselves.

Since a state is always a class organization directed against another class, the workers' state as a repressive tool of class rule would gradually "wither away." At the very least, there would be no secret police, no national guard, no standing army, and no immigration authorities. Furthermore, since politics is essentially the struggle of members of one class against another, political practice as we know it today would not exist in a communist society.

Beyond these few generalizations, there is not much more we today can say about a communist society without risking uneducated guesses.

The professional mouthpieces of capitalist ruling classes seldom argue that the communist goal of a classless society is undesirable. Their more usual strategy is to ridicule such a society as unrealistic "pie in the sky." According to the capitalists, Marxists dream of creating Heaven on Earth, a new Garden of Eden, or a science fiction paradise of complete equality, harmony, and bliss.

Even from the brief discussion in this chapter, it should be clear that Marxists do not fight for anything of the sort. One does not have to believe in creating Heaven on Earth to recognize that it is possible to fight and win against an international capitalist system that condemns the greater part of humanity to grinding poverty, deadening routine, hunger, disease, and oppression, while the wealthiest rulers of the wealthiest states continue to squander untold human energy and precious resources on trillion-dollar military machines and weapons of mass destruction.

There are no "iron laws of history" that guarantee the eventual triumph of socialism and communism. The threat of nuclear, biological, or chemical holocaust; the proliferation of conventional wars on one hundred different battlefields; desperate poverty; chauvinism; and national and religious differences—any or all of these may continue to divide workers, women, and oppressed peoples and lead to an ever-tighter global tyranny of capital. Indeed, irreversible damage to our global environment may place the very continuity of our species in danger. These dangers, and perhaps dangers yet unforeseen, may prevent communism from ever being achieved.

Historical materialism allows us to understand social change in a scientific manner. But truth alone will not set us free. Over a century and a half ago, Karl Marx wrote that "theory, too, will become a material force as soon as it seizes the masses."[14] In order for the most militant workers to lead their class down the long road of revolution, they need to take a firm grip on the weapon of Marxist theory and unite historical materialism with a party of fighting thinkers and thinking fighters. Once we recognize this, we will have taken the first step toward what Bertolt Brecht called militant learning.

Summary

Key terms discussed in this chapter include *socialism, communism, dictatorship of the proletariat,* and *workers' councils*.

Socialism is a period of transition between two sorts of society: capitalist society and communist society. This period of transition is characterized by the state power of workers, rather than capitalists. Since workers and their families outnumber capitalists, the demand for socialism is a demand for much greater democracy. Under socialism distribution of the means of subsistence and all manner of goods and services would take place according to the slogan "To each according to labor contributed."

Communism, by contrast, is a possible future mode of production. In a communist society, production would be for use instead of the market, and distribution would take place according to the slogan

"To each according to need." Beyond a few general remarks, there is not much more I can safely say about this, the most distant goal for which Marxists fight.

Reading List

*Engels, Friedrich. *Socialism, Utopian and Scientific*. New York: International Publishers, 1935. This was originally the third and final part of Engels's book *Anti-Duhring*, first published in 1878. It is largely an account of the earliest socialist thinkers and experimenters in Europe at the beginning of the industrial revolution, their failures and their influence on the founders of historical materialism.

*Marx, Karl. *Critique of the Gotha Program*. New York: International Publishers, 1938. Marx's criticisms, originally written in the margins of the 1875 draft program for the unification of the Marxist Social Democratic Workers' Party with a non-Marxist party, to form the German Social-Democratic Party. Marx emphasized the importance of a well-disciplined, tightly organized party and the necessity of workers' power after the revolution. He also outlined the main features of the transition from capitalism to communism and distinguished the higher stage of communism (which I have referred to simply as *communism*) from the lower stage of communism (which I have referred to as *socialism*). It is interesting to note that Marx's criticisms were not taken to heart by the party officials.

Elizabeth Gurley Flynn (1890–1964)

Ho Chi Minh (1890–1969)

Che Guevara (1928–1967)

Three Fighting Marxists

Elizabeth Gurley Flynn (1890–1964)

A second-generation Irish-American from a working-class background, Elizabeth Gurley Flynn became a socialist speaker in New York City at the age of sixteen, a strike organizer for the International Workers of the World (the IWW), a Communist leader, and a lifelong feminist. She was sixty-two years old in February 1953, when she was sentenced to three years in prison for violating the thought-control Smith Act.

The character of the U.S. working class has changed greatly since 1912, when Flynn and the IWW led textile workers on a mass strike in Lawrence, Massachusetts. Labor leaders long ago abandoned the goal of workers' power, and many of the most important gains for which workers in the United States sacrificed, fought, and in some cases even died have been lost in recent decades. Labor unions have come under increasing attack and membership has fallen; heavy industries have closed down or moved abroad; temporary and part-time workers now make up a large part of the workforce; the average number of breadwinners per household has grown, although the average size of a household has shrunk; real wages have slipped, and the gap between rich and poor has grown. In spite of the changes, however, workers in the United States face the same opponent that Flynn, Eugene Debs, Mother Jones, Joe Hill, and other working-class leaders faced in their day—big business, or more accurately, U.S. monopoly capital.

Ho Chi Minh (1890–1969)

Ho Chi Minh devoted his life to the struggle to free his country, Vietnam, from foreign domination and to build a better life for the Vietnamese people. As a journalist, an organizer, and a political leader, "Uncle Ho" led an impoverished people to victory against the vastly superior military might of Japanese, French, and U.S. invaders. These victories, however, did not come easily. The United States alone dropped more bombs on the small country of Vietnam than were dropped by both sides during World War II. Over the course of four decades of war, nearly 2 million Vietnamese men, women, and children lost their lives before they finally defeated the last of the imperialist invaders in the spring of 1975.

Ho spent much time in prison, where he sometimes wrote poetry. While a prisoner in China in 1942 he wrote: "Let the prison doors open and the real dragon will fly out."[15] Engels once complained that Marx had sewn dragon's teeth, but so far no dragons had sprouted from those seeds. "Uncle Ho," the kindly old wisp of a man with homemade sandals on his feet, was a real dragon.

Che Guevara (1928–1967)

In December 1956 a small but determined group of guerrillas led by a young Cuban, Dr. Fidel Castro y Ruiz, landed on a beach near a cane field in Cuba's Oriente Province. Among them was a young Argentinian, Ernesto "Che" Guevara. On New Year's Eve 1959, after two years of fighting in the mountains, the guerrillas led by Castro and Guevara entered the city of Havana and drove the pro-U.S. dictator of Cuba off the island. Since then Fidel

Castro and the vast majority of the Cuban people have stood up against ever more vicious U.S. attacks and economic embargo aimed at destroying Cuban independence and blocking attempts to improve the lives of the Cuban people.

In 1961, Che became Cuba's Minister of Industry, but in 1965 he sent a letter to Castro, informing him of his intention to continue to fight for the independence of Latin America. In November 1966 he arrived in Bolivia to organize the guerrilla movement there. In October 1967 his group was attacked by CIA-trained troops. Che was wounded, captured, and then murdered in cold blood. A few months before his death, a news service in Cuba released a message from Che, which ended with the following words: "Wherever death may surprise us, let it be welcome, as long as our battle cry has reached even one receptive ear, and another hand reaches out to take up our arms, and others come forward to join our funeral dirge with the clattering of machine guns and new calls for battle and for victory."[16]

Notes

1. One that, evidently, can be reversed.

2. Marx's letter to Arnold Ruge, dated September 1843, is quoted in Robert C. Tucker, ed., *The Marx-Engels Reader* (New York: W. W. Norton and Company, 1972), p. 8.

3. Friedrich Engels, *Anti-Duhring* (New York: International Publishers, 1939), pp. 304–305.

4. V.I. Lenin, *The State and Revolution* (New York: International Publishers, 1932), p. 77.

5. Friedrich Engels, *The Origin of the Family, Private Property and the State* (New York: International Publishers, 1972), p. 129.

6. V.I. Lenin, *The Teachings of Karl Marx* (New York: International Publishers, 1930), p. 30.

7. V.I. Lenin, *The Teachings of Karl Marx*.

8. Citation from David McLellan, *Karl Marx: Selected Writings* (Oxford: Oxford University Press, 1977), p. 296.

9. David McLellan, *Karl Marx: Selected Writings,* p. 237.

10. Rosa Luxemburg, *The Russian Revolution and Leninism or Marxism?* (Ann Arbor: University of Michigan Press, 1961), p. 71.

11. V.I. Lenin, *Collected Works* Vol. 33 (Moscow: Progress Publishers, 1966), p. 225.

12. In this regard, Article 6 of the 1977 Constitution of the USSR was terribly regrettable. This article guaranteed that the Communist Party would determine "... the general perspectives of the development of society and the course of the domestic and foreign policy of the USSR ... and the great constructive work of the Soviet people."

13. McLellan, *Karl Marx*, p. 569.
14. McLellan, *Karl Marx*, p. 69.
15. Ho Chi Minh, *Prison Diary* sixth edition (Hanoi: Foreign Languages Publishing House, 1978), p. 86.
16. "Message to the Tricontinental," published on April 16, 1967. Reprinted in Ernesto Che Guevara, *Che Guevara and the Cuban Revolution: Writings and Speeches of Ernesto Che Guevara* (Sydney: Pathfinder, 1987), p. 360.

Glossary

Note: Terms that appear in this glossary followed by an asterisk (*) are included as entries in the glossary.

Alienation. A state of affairs in which, according to some Marxists, the products of our hands and brains seem to confront us as hostile forces and our communities and even our own personalities appear fragmented, threatening, and divided against themselves. This state of affairs is characteristic of capitalism, with its wage labor, highly specialized division of labor, and operation of powerful market forces.

Bolshevik Revolution. The working-class revolution led by Lenin's Bolshevik Party in Russia in November 1917 (or October of that year, according to the old Russian calendar). Also called the October Revolution and distinguished from the March 1917 revolution that overthrew the Czar and resulted in the establishment of what came to be called the Provisional Government.

Bourgeois Rights. Legal and moral claims based on the general belief, characteristic of *commodity** production, that a person has a rightful claim to property because he or she has exchanged an equal *value** for it. Contrasted to the notion that a person has a right to goods or services because of birth (as in feudal *societies**) or need (as in *communist** societies). In addition to the right to hold private property, bourgeois rights include equal representation under the law, freedom of expression, and other rights of individuals.

Bureaucracy. Administrators and other mid-level employees of a *state** (typically of a capitalist or socialist state) who form a social stratum, or "caste," that enjoys privileges such as job security, official authority, or relatively high salaries.

Capital. A social relation characteristic of the highest form of *commodity** production, in which *surplus value** is produced for private appropriation. Viewed more narrowly in terms of the process of production, capital is a portion of surplus value that is plowed back into production. Constant capital is the *means of production** used up in the course of production that is embodied unchanged in the value of the final product. Variable capital, or

133

capital expended for *labor-power*,* expands in the *labor** process, creating surplus value.

Capitalism. A *mode of production** characterized by *commodity** production and *exploitation** through *wage labor.**

Class. A large group that differs from other such groups in a *society** in the following four ways: (1) the place it occupies in a given *mode of production**; (2) its relationship to possession, legal ownership, or control of the *means of production**; (3) its ability or inability to appropriate a surplus product, in a manner determined by a given mode of production; and (4) the share of total social wealth its members have at their disposal.

Commodity. A good produced for exchange, rather than immediate consumption by those who produced it, or for the satisfaction of social needs. *Capitalism** is the highest stage of development of commodity production.

Communism. A possible *mode of production** characterized by a high level of productivity of *labor*,* an absence of conflicting *classes*,* and the disappearance of the *state** as a repressive tool of class rule. Communism also refers to a *society** dominated by the communist mode of production. ("Primitive communism," or "communalism," is a mode of production characterized by a level of productivity of labor too low to permit widespread and systematic *exploitation.**)

Dialectic, "Laws" of. Very general observations that can be restated as at least three methodological principles or rules of thumb: (1) Everything the sciences study changes. Everything about which we know has a history; (2) change is not always gradual or just tick-tock repetitions of past changes. Sometimes changes take place very rapidly, or even as explosions, and as a result entirely new qualities (characteristics or properties), objects, and processes appear; (3) change in one thing often causes change in other things. Therefore, in order to view something dialectically, we should see it as part of an interconnected whole in which every part is related to and determined by every other part. These principles are valuable because they direct our attention to aspects of a wide variety of things and processes that might otherwise be overlooked.

Dictatorship of the Proletariat. The first stage of workers' power, during and immediately after the smashing of the bourgeois *state.** (Refer to Marx's "Letter to Weydemeyer," 1852, quoted by Lenin in *The State and Revolution:* "The transition from capitalism to Communism will certainly bring a great variety and abundance of political forms, but the essence will inevitably be only one: *the dictatorship of the proletariat.*" Also compare to the entry for *Socialism** in this glossary.)

Glossary

Economic Structure. The combination of the various *relations of production** which are established within a given *society.** The economic structure of any given *class** society usually includes more than one *mode of production.** For example, feudalism may coexist with capitalism within a given economic structure. Nevertheless, there is almost always a politically and economically dominant mode of production. Within most societies, relations of production conforming to the dominant mode of production modify relations of production conforming to subordinate modes of production.

Exchange-Value (or Value). The value that a useful thing has irrespective of its particular qualities or makeup or the particular needs and wants it satisfies. Exchange-value appears first as a ratio in which a certain number or measure of useful things of one kind is equated with a certain number or measure of useful things of another kind (for example, four loaves of bread might be equated with one cotton shirt). Exchange-value is measured in units of time necessary on the average to produce a *commodity.**

Exploitation. In the most general terms, the appropriation of a surplus product from those who produced it. Exploitation takes place when a non-producer (who is not part of the household of a producer, or a worker's dependent) systematically takes part of the surplus product that others have produced. With the exception of communalism and *communism,** each *mode of production** has its own particular form of exploitation. Under *capitalism,** exploitation takes the form of private expropriation of *surplus value** from workers through *wage labor.**

Extended Reproduction. Takes place when a portion of the annual total social product is not consumed, but rather is accumulated to increase the capacity of production.

Finance Capital. Refer to the entry for *imperialism** in this glossary.

Hegemony. The manner in which a *class** and its allies typically struggle for political power today. Hegemony involves two funtions: (1) domination by a ruling class of those who are ruled, and to a lesser extent, of *society** as a whole; and (2) leadership of a class and the allies of that class by its most politically and intellectually active members. Leadership is necessary if a revolutionary class is to win *state** power; both domination and leadership are necessary if a ruling class is to hold on to state power. Gramsci recognized that, especially in modern societies, political domination cannot succeed for long if it relies only on force and not on the consent of the majority. Thus, *ideology** is as important to political domination as it is to political leadership.

Historical Materialism. The science founded by Karl Marx that takes history—or more precisely, the constitution of *modes of production**—as its unique object of investigation.

Ideology. The usual "lived relationship" of an individual, a *class,** or a *society** as a whole. Most people remain unaware of the ideologies to which they adhere and that partially define who they think they are.

Imperialism. The monopoly stage of *capitalism.** Lenin pointed to five defining features of imperialism: (1) The concentration of production and *capital** develops to such an extent that it creates monopolies, which play a decisive role in economic life; (2) the merging of industrial capital with banking capital, resulting in the creation of *finance capital**; (3) the importance of capital transfer, as contrasted to the export of *commodities**; (4) the formation of international capitalist monopolies, or transnational corporations, which share the globe among themselves; and (5) the complete territorial division of the globe into spheres of interest (at first through direct colonial domination, then through neocolonialism) by the most powerful capitalist *states.**

Infrastructure (or "economic base"). The unity of *productive forces** and *relations of production** within a *society.** Traditionally, the infrastructure is contrasted with the *superstructure,** which consists very roughly of ideological *practices** and some institutions of the *state.** To avoid misunderstandings, it is important to remember that these terms, infrastructure and superstructure, are metaphors. They are not to be taken literally. The point of the metaphor is that the superstructure could not "stay up" without the infrastructure.

Labor. Purposeful activity, or expenditure of skills and energy, without which production cannot take place. Labor is the *use-value** of *labor-power.**

Labor-Power. The capacity or power to work (the strength of producers, together with their skills and technical knowledge), which workers sell for wages. Labor-power differs from *labor,** which is labor-power's *use-value.** Under *capitalism,** labor-power is a *commodity.**

Labor Theory of Value. According to this theory, the value of *labor-power** in exchange is the average socially necessary *labor** time required to reproduce it.

Law of Value. The principle that *commodities** tend to be produced and exchanged according to the average, socially necessary (abstract) *labor** expended in making them. According to Marx, the magnitude of the value of any article is the amount of labor socially necessary, or the labor time socially necessary, for its production. (Refer to the entries for *Value** and *Labor** in this glossary.)

Market Relations. Social relations in which buyers confront sellers, *commodities** are exchanged for money, and money is exchanged for commodities.

Materialism. Refer to the discussion in the first section of Chapter 1.

Materialist Dialectics. Refer to the entry for *Dialectics, Laws of,** in this glossary. Materialist dialectics differs from other dialectical schools of thought, such as G.W.F. Hegel's, which view the various parts of a whole (or a "totality") as expressions or reflections of a single, simple essence. Thus, for example, Hegel—who saw the modern *state** as the totality of human life, and the individual as an expression of the state—concluded that only as a member of a state is a person a genuine individual. Contrast this view to the discussion of the state in Chapter 4 of this text.

Means of Consumption. That part of wages and profit that is withdrawn from the process of production of *surplus value** to be consumed. "Consumer goods."

Means of Production. The land, forests, waters, mineral resources, and raw materials that are necessary for economic production to take place, together with instruments of production, production sites, plants, factories, computers, offices, means of transportation, communication, information storage and retrieval, and so on.

Mode of Production. Certain *productive forces** in combination with certain *relations of production.** In Chapter 2 it was emphasized that often more than one mode of production exists within a *society.** Broadly speaking, the various modes of production that have existed may be characterized as communal, slave, feudal, and capitalist. Marx did not consider this to be a hard-and-fast schema, however. He also mentioned another mode of production, the Asiatic or tributary mode of production, which has characterized a variety of societies, from ancient China and India to the Aztec and Inca empires. *Communism** is a possible mode of production characterized by a high level of productivity of *labor,** together with the absence of widespread *exploitation,** *market relations,** and conflicting *classes.**

Necessary Labor Time. The part of a given period of work such as a workday, during which workers produce products with a *value** equal to the bundle of goods they consume to: (a) reproduce their *labor-power** for another such period of work, and (b) raise, educate, and train a future generation of workers. (Refer to the entry for *Surplus Labor Time** in this glossary.)

Neocolonialism. The indirect *exploitation** of peoples within the borders of officially independent *states** by means of unbalanced trade relations, the export of *capital** on terms unfavorable to those on the receiving end, manipulation of the terms of trade and "development aid." In order to prop up neocolonialism, the ex-colonial powers resort to threats of military intervention, and "native" rulers rely on particularly brutal police forces and armies to thwart democratic movements.

Paris Commune. In March 1871, workers in Paris revolted against the regime of Louis Bonaparte and seized power in the city. The new workers' government, or commune, abolished private property, established new democratic institutions for workers' self-rule, and undertook to defend the city against the French army's seige. After holding out for a little more than two months, the French bourgeoisie joined forces with its long-time German "enemy," to attack and defeat the commune, killing 30,000 men, women, and children in the process. In spite of the defeat of the Paris Commune, Marx pointed to the commune as the first example of the *dictatorship of the proletariat.** (Refer to the entry for *Bolshevik Revolution** in this glossary.)

Practice. In the most general terms, a practice is a systematic or repeated collective activity. Practices make up and determine the character of a *society.** Some (but not all) practices involve transforming raw materials into products by means of *labor** and *means of production.** In *class** societies, these include (but are not limited to) economic, ideological, and political practices.

Price. According to Marx, the price of a *commodity** is its *value** expressed in money; price is the money name of the labor realized in a commodity. (The precise relationship between value and price, however, is very controversial among Marxists today.)

Productive Forces. Tools, techniques, and knowledge with which humans make materials usable, together with the workforce and natural resources. The productive forces include: (1) all *means of production** including natural resources; (2) *labor-power**; (3) scientific and technological applications for productive activity including systems of organization of workers within a productive unit.

Relations of (Economic) Production. Relations of control over people, *labor-power,** raw materials, or *productive forces** during the course of economic production. Relations of production include: (1) legal relations of property ownership—contracts, laws regulating commerce, patents, copyrights, and so on; (2) control of the *means of production**—for example, the relationship between managers and workers within a firm, or relations between productive units such as individual factories within an industry; and (3) relationships between productive units within an international system of production.

Socialism. A period of transition between two *modes of production,** *capitalism** and *communism.** Socialism is workers' power—that is, a state of affairs in which wage earners and other direct producers engaged in economically productive activity constitute the ruling *class,** and the *state,** in this sense, is a workers' state. (Compare to the entry for *Communism** in this glossary.)

Socially Necessary Labor. The average, socially prescribed *labor** time required for the production of a given item.

Society/Social Formation. A whole composed of a system of economic production plus various other *practices** including ideological practice.

Soviet. The Russian word for "council." During the *Bolshevik Revolution** and in the years immediately after it, soviets made up of workers, peasants, and soldiers were a means of democratically exercising *state** power at the grassroots level. Hundreds of soviets throughout Russia and elsewhere discussed issues, decided on a course of action, and proceeded to carry out those decisions themselves. In addition, elected representatives or deputies from the soviets met from time to time to communicate and coordinate policies affecting the Soviet Union as a whole. Later, however, during the reign of Joseph Stalin, the soviets were transformed into a top-down mechanism for one-party dictatorship.

The State.

In *The Origin of the Family, Private Property and the State,* Engels described the state as

> a product of society at a certain stage of development; it is the admission that this society has become entangled in an insoluble contradiction with itself, that it is cleft into irreconcilable antagonisms which it is powerless to dispel. But in order that these antagonisms, classes with conflicting economic interests, may not consume themselves and society in sterile struggles, a power apparently standing above society becomes necessary, whose purpose is to moderate the conflict and keep it within the bounds of "order"; and this power arising out of society, but placing itself above it, and increasingly separating itself from it, is the state.

(New York: International Publishers, 1972, p. 229.)

State Capitalism. *State** ownership of the *means of production,** combined with the private appropriation of *surplus value** through *wage labor.**

Superstructure. Economic and political *practices** of social production. (Refer to the entry for *Infrastructure** in this glossary.)

Surplus Labor Time. The part of a given period of work such as a workday during which workers work to produce goods whose *value** exceeds the value of the goods workers consume. (Compare to the entry for *Necessary Labor Time** in this glossary.)

Surplus Value. The difference between the *value** of the product of labor and the value of *labor-power**; the difference between what the capitalist pays for labor-power and the value that the use of this labor-power adds to the value of the *commodities*.* Under *capitalism*,* surplus value is appropriated by the capitalist and distributed in the forms of interest, rent, and profit.

Unity of Opposites. Things and structures that at first may appear to be stable and unchanging, but are actually made up of opposing parts and depend for their unity and development on this very opposition of their parts. Something viewed as a whole, such as a *class** *society*,* that is held together and develops not in spite of but rather because of the fact that it is made up of conflicting or opposing forces.

Use-Value. The reason some object or service is wanted. Examples are: the nutritional content of bread; the nice smell of perfume; *labor*,* with reference to *labor-power**; or the fact that, thanks to advertising, wearing a certain style of shoe enhances one's feeling of self-importance. The non-exchange usefulness or desirability of any given object or service, whether or not it is a product of human labor. Use-value is determined by socially, historically, and individually variable needs.

Value. Refer to the entry for *Exchange-Value** in this glossary.

Wage Labor. Work performed for a wage in the service of a private employer who, because the employer owns or controls the *means of production*,* is able to appropriate and dispose of whatever surplus the workers produce.

About the Book and Author

Though Marxism has been declared dead many times, it remains vital as a theory of social and political change as we move into the twenty-first century. Concise and accessible, this book will introduce undergraduates in various disciplines and others unfamiliar with Marxism to the basic vocabulary of Marx's thought.

Using engaging examples, Markar Melkonian emphasizes Marxism as a materialist approach to understanding society and human history. Drawing on the work of V.I. Lenin, Rosa Luxemburg, Antonio Gramsci, and more recent figures, Melkonian introduces such concepts as social practice, mode of production, class, state power, ideological hegemony, and imperialism. A glossary and end-of-chapter reading lists provide beginning students with additional guidance.

For more advanced students looking for a lean but sophisticated overview, this book constitutes a trenchant and engaging reevaluation of Marx's intellectual legacy.

Markar Melkonian is a filmmaker, veteran solidarity worker, and graduate of the Department of Philosophy at the University of Massachusetts at Amherst. In his teens, he joined the United Farmworkers' campaign to organize field-workers in California's San Joaquin Valley. Since then he has been a member of the Iranian Students Association, the Lebanese National Movement, and the Palestinian resistance as well as a volunteer worker in Nicaragua. He is currently active in the San Francisco-based Sardarabad Collective, an Armenian solidarity group.

Index

Note: Items in this index that are followed by an asterisk (*) are included as separate entries in the Glossary (pp. 133–140).

Accumulation of Capital (R. Luxemburg), 68
Africa, 38, 46, 47, 96, 97, 99, 100, 101, 102
  central and southern, 39
  communal societies in, 71–72
  eastern, 55
  Marxists of, 109–110
  North, 40
  pollution in, 105
  scramble for, 97
  See also African Party for the Independence of Guinea and Cape Verde; Afro-Shirazi Party; Angola; Apartheid; Cameroon; Congolese National Movement; Ghana; Guinea; Egypt; Morocco; Mozambique; Rodney, W.; South Africa; Sudan; Zambia; Zanzibar
African Party for the Independence of Guinea and Cape Verde, 110
Afro-Shirazi Party (Zanzibar), 109–110
Alienation,* 60–61, 65, 67, 133.
  See also Labor,* alienated
Amazon Basin, 36, 105, 122
Angola, 110
Anti-Duhring (F. Engels), 9, 66, 115, 129
Apartheid, 78
Arabs, 79

Aral Sea, 106
Argentina, 95
Aristocracy of labor. *See* Labor,* aristocracy of
Asia, 47, 97, 99, 100, 101, 102
  Central, 106
  Southeast, 36
  See also China; India; Japan; Korea; Siberia; Sri Lanka; Philippines; Vietnam
"Asiatic" mode of production. *See* Mode of production,* "Asiatic"
Australia, 96
  Aborigines of, 36
Aztec Empire, 39

Baran, Paul, 108
Ben Barka, 109
Berberoghlu, Berch, 108–109
Big Bang, 10
Big business, 82–86, 87, 96, 99, 107, 130
Bolivia, 131
Bolshevik Revolution* (October Revolution), 68–69, 120, 124, 133, 139. *See also* Bolsheviks; Lenin
Bolsheviks, 68, 124, 133. *See also* Lenin, V.I.; Luxemburg, R.; Bolshevik Revolution*
Bonaparte, Louis Napoleon, 138
Bourgeoisie, 56, 71, 76
  dictatorship of the, 123

143

French, 138
　　See also Capitalism;* Class*
Bourgeois rights,* 126–127, 133
Brazil. See Amazon Basin
Brecht, Bertolt, 4, 128
British Museum, 23
Brown Brothers, 99
Buddhism, 89(n7)
Bukharin, Nikolai, 49
Bureaucracy,* 5, 46, 133
　　and centralism, 49
　　federal, 84
　　and socialism,* 119, 124
Business cycle, 63
Butler, Smedley D., 98–99

Cabral, Amilcar, 110
Cape Verde, 110
Capital,* 46, 61–65, 80, 91, 93, 95, 96, 97–98, 128, 133–134
　　accumulation of, 62, 65, 103
　　concentration of, 47, 93, 108, 122, 136
　　constant, 62, 65, 92
　　export of, 97–98, 100, 108, 137
　　finance, 96, 100, 107, 108, 135, 136. See also Capitalism,* monopoly; Imperialism*
　　formation, 100
　　gains taxes, 119
　　industrial, 92, 96, 136
　　organic composition of, 62
　　variable, 62, 65, 92
　　See also Money
Capital (K. Marx), 7, 9, 23, 24, 29, 48, 50, 55, 64, 66, 67, 94, 105, 121, 136
Capitalism,* 4, 18, 34, 41, 47, 48, 60, 65, 67, 79, 83, 92, 93, 97, 127–128, 134, 135, 136, 140
　　advanced, 5, 16, 65, 101, 103, 115, 122
　　in Africa, 109

and commodity production, 51, 57
in England, 23, 32
and exploitation,* 5, 55–60, 66, 135
and family relations, 121
free exchange, 94
industrial, 1, 136
international, 96–103, 108
as a mode of production,* 39, 40, 42, 46, 51–70, 114, 137, 138
monopoly, 40, 91–96, 98, 99, 101, 105, 107, 130, 136
and planning, 115
and pollution, 105
and socialism,* 117–118, 123, 126, 129, 134
See also Capitalist societies; Capitalists; Imperialism;* Mode of production;* Capitalism,* monopoly; State,* capitalist; State capitalism*
Capitalists, 41, 42, 43–44, 45, 56, 57, 58, 60, 62, 63, 64, 66, 85, 91, 93, 95, 96, 97, 120, 123, 127, 136, 139–140
　　big, 44, 82, 91, 92, 93, 104
　　as a class,* 43, 44, 51, 56, 61, 64, 65, 76, 82, 92, 96, 114, 124
　　and feudalism, 4
　　ideology* of, 23, 68, 80, 83
　　merchants, 4, 73
　　and productive labor, 116
　　and rate of profit, 16
　　as rulers, 74, 76, 77, 78, 82, 85–86, 87, 89, 96, 118, 123–124, 127. See also State,* and class rule
　　See also Capitalism;* Capitalist societies; Mode of production;* State,* and capitalism;* State capitalism*
Capitalist societies, 1, 16, 27, 30, 34, 37, 39, 40, 41, 42, 44, 51,

Index

55, 56, 63, 64, 66, 76, 79, 82, 84, 92, 96, 101, 103, 107, 108, 115, 128
   division of labor in, 119
   See also Capitalism;* Capitalists; Mode of production;* State,* and capitalism; State capitalism*
Capone, Al, 99
Carnegie, Andrew, 51
Cartel, 94, 103
Castro, Fidel, 103, 130, 131
Central Asia. See Aral Sea; Asia, Central
Central Intelligence Agency (CIA), 109, 110, 131
Chile, 78
China, 39, 99, 102, 130
Chipko (environmental movement), 122
Christianity, 89(n7)
CIA. See Central Intelligence Agency
Civil society, 82–83
Civil War in France, The (K. Marx), 8, 88
Class,* 30, 40–46, 46–47, 81, 134
   capitalist, 4, 5, 23, 38, 55–56, 61, 73, 75, 76, 77, 83, 92. See also Capitalists, as a class*
   dictatorship, 123, 124
   divisions, 31, 35, 40–41, 44–45, 78, 86, 127
   hegemony,* 74–75, 76, 86, 87, 135
   and ideology,* 136
   Lenin's definition of, 42–43
   middle, 45, 46, 81, 92
   relations, 16
   revolutionary, 74, 135
   rule, 13, 74, 77–78, 80, 85, 87, 134. See also State,* and class rule
   ruling, 16, 17, 37, 71–77, 80, 81, 82, 85, 86, 87, 96, 98, 116, 123, 124, 127, 135, 138.
   See also Big business; Finance capital;* Monopoly capitalism
   society,* 33, 41, 45, 82, 113, 125, 127, 135, 138, 140
   structure, 46, 92
   struggle, 4, 7, 13, 41, 43, 64–65, 72, 75, 83, 88, 114, 118, 127, 134, 137, 139
   women and, 120–121
   working, 45, 47, 49, 67, 76, 77, 92, 101, 103, 104, 107, 114, 115, 125, 126, 129, 130, 133
   See also Big business; Capitalists; Feudalism
Class Struggles in France, The (K. Marx), 123
Cold War, 17, 79, 103
Colonialism. See Neocolonialism*
Committee on Economic Development, 84
Commodity,* 51–55, 56, 103, 122, 134, 136
   and capitalism,* 57–65, 91, 95–97, 101
   export of, 97, 108, 136
   labor-power* as a, 58–59, 66, 136
   production, 36, 46, 51–55, 56, 57, 65, 126–127, 133, 134
   value of, 57–65, 66, 135, 138, 139–140
   See also Capitalism,* and commodity production; Labor-power;* Law of value;* Money;* Price;* Use-value;* Exchange-value*
Communal societies ("primitive communalism"), 35–36, 37, 39, 71–72, 121, 134, 135, 137. See also Communism;* Mode of production*
Communism,* 107, 113, 115, 117, 118, 120, 123, 125–128,

128–129, 133, 134, 135, 137, 138
"Scientific," 2
socialism* and, 113–114, 115, 116, 127, 128
See also Communal societies; Mode of production;* Utopian socialists
Communist League, 47
Communist Manifesto (K. Marx and F. Engels), 9, 47, 67, 71
Communist Party, 46, 77, 124
of Germany, 68
of Italy, 88
of South Africa. See South African Communist Party
of the Soviet Union (USSR), 110
of Sudan, 110
See also Communists; Bolsheviks
Concentration
of capital, 47, 93, 95, 108, 122, 136
of production, 93, 94, 95, 107, 108, 136
Condition of the Working Class in England, The (F. Engels), 23
Conglomerate, 95
Congolese National Movement, 109
Congress of the United States, 44–45, 84
Constitution of the USSR, 131(n12)
Contradiction. See Dialectical contradiction
Corporation, 43, 44, 45, 84, 93–96, 105, 106, 107, 109, 136
Council on Foreign Relations, 84
Critique of Political Economy (K. Marx), 32, 39, 48
Critique of the Gotha Program (K. Marx), 10, 115, 125–126, 129
Crusades, 73

Cuba, 99, 104, 130–131
Czar, 133

Darwin, Charles, 18, 19–20, 21
Debs, Eugene, 130
DeMan, Henri, 3
Demand. See Effective demand; Supply and demand
Democracy, 49, 68–69, 75, 80, 86, 98, 120, 123–125, 128
R. Luxemburg on, 69
Democratic centralism, 49
Democratic Party, 84
Descartes, Rene, 13, 14, 22
Determinism. See Technological determinism
Dialectic, "laws" of,* 19, 21, 23, 41, 134. See also Materialist dialectics,* 137
Dictatorship of the proletariat,* 123–124, 128, 134, 138
Dominican Republic, 99
Dos Santos, Marcelino, 110

Earth (the planet), 9, 10, 15, 19, 127
Economic and Philosophic Manuscripts of 1844 (K. Marx), 60–61
Economic structure,* 30, 32, 135
Effective demand, 63, 65, 98, 103
Egypt, 34, 39
Eighteenth Brumaire of Louis Bonaparte (K. Marx), 8, 88
Eisenhower, Dwight D., 103–104
Engels, Friedrich (or Frederick)
and *Anti-Duhring*, 9, 66, 115, 129
biographical note on, 23–24
on communism,* 120, 126
and *The Communist Manifesto*, 9, 47, 67, 71
and *The Condition of the Working Class in England*, 23

Index

on the environment, 105
and *The German Ideology*, 48
and *Ludwig Feuerbach and the Outcome of Classical German Philosophy*, 22
on Marx, 88, 130
on nature, 9
and *The Origin of the Family, Private Property and the State*, 87
and other writings of, 8, 9, 16, 47, 123
and *Socialism, Utopian and Scientific*, 129
and "Speech at the Graveside of Karl Marx," 22
on the state,* 74, 75–76, 77, 86, 139
on *Theses on Feuerbach* (K. Marx), 23
See also Mayer, Gustav; Marx, Karl; State*
England. *See* Great Britain
Enlightenment, 9
Environmentalism, 5, 104–107, 108, 120, 121–123, 128
Europe, 55, 97, 98, 101, 102
  eastern, 49, 82, 103, 106, 113, 114
  feudalism in, 39–40
  medieval, 34, 38, 73, 107, 129
  southern, 4
  western, 84, 87
  See also Great Britain; France; Greece; Italy
European Economic Community, 109
Exchange-value,* 52–54, 57, 59, 61–62, 64, 65, 135
  and bourgeois right,* 133
  of labor power,* 59, 64, 66, 117, 136, 137, 139–140
  and money, 69(n3)

and prices of production, 55, 138
and surplus value,* 58–60
transfer of, 101
See also Commodity;* Law of value;* Market, relations;* Price;* Surplus value;* Use-value*
Exploitation,* 13, 40, 41, 43, 46–47, 65, 135
  absence of, 71–72, 113–114, 116, 127, 137
  capitalist, 5, 44, 55–60, 64, 66, 76, 105, 134
  and class rule, 87
  definition of, 37, 43
  feudal, 38
  and imperialism,* 68, 80, 100–101, 106, 109, 137
  opposition to, 81, 83
  rate of, 60, 93
  and socialism,* 118
  and the state,* 73–74, 78
  and women, 120
  See also Capitalism;* Class;* Imperialism;* Feudalism; Labor;* Labor-power;* Profit;* Superprofits; Surplus labor time;* Surplus value;* Wage labor;* Wages
Extended reproduction,* 135

Federal Bureau of Investigation (FBI), 86
Feudalism, 1, 32, 39–40, 41, 46, 73, 107, 133
  as a mode of production,* 38, 40, 135, 137
  and rulers, 4, 38, 43, 56, 73, 78
  and the state,* 87
  See also Bourgeoisie; Capitalism;* Class;* Crusades; Mode of production*
Fichte, Johann, 11

Finance capital,* 91, 96, 100, 107, 108, 135, 136. *See also* Big business; Capital;* Imperialism;* Monopoly capitalism
First International, 24
Flew, Anthony, 23
Flynn, Elizabeth Gurley, 76–77, 129–130
Fourier, Charles, 114
France, 92
　civil wars in, 8
　as a "Great Power," 96, 97
　Marx on, 88
　revolution in, 73
France, Anatole, 78–79
FRELIMO, 110
French Revolution. *See* France, revolution in
Friedrich Engels: A Biography (G. Mayer), 24

Galilei, Galileo, 4, 16
Garang, Joseph, 110
Garden of Eden, 127
Genesis, 15
German Federal Republic, 69
German Ideology (K. Marx and F. Engels), 48
German Social Democratic Party, 67, 129
Germany, 75, 78, 123
　as a "Great Power," 96, 97
　Marx on, 47
　revolution in, 24, 69
　workers in, 92
Ghana, 102
Glorious Revolution, 32
God, 9–10, 15, 51, 75, 78, 81
Gorbachev, Mikhail, 120
Gramsci, Antonio
　biographical note on, 88–89
　on communism,* 120
　on hegemony,* 74–75, 77–78, 87, 135
　and *Letters from Prison*, 89
　on socialism,* 115
　and *State and Civil Society*, 87
　and "The Study of Philosophy," 22
　See also Hegemony;* Ideology;* State*
Great Britain, 23, 32, 47, 73, 92, 96, 97
Great Depression, 76, 103
"Great Powers," 97–99
Greece, 34
Grenada, 104
Grundrisse (K. Marx), 48
Guatemala, 78
Guevara, Ernesto Che, 130–131
Guinea, 110

Haiti, 99
Hanga, Abdullah Kassim, 109
Hani, Chris, 110
Havana, 130
Hegel, G.W.F., 21, 48, 137
Hegemony,* 74–75, 76, 80, 86, 87, 101, 135. *See also* Gramsci, A.; Ideology*
Hill, Joe, 130
Hinduism, 2
Historical materialism*
　and communism,* 113, 115, 125, 129
　and conspiracy theories, 85
　and environmentalism, 106
　as a guide to action, 107, 128
　and ideology,* 80
　Lenin on, 48
　and Marx and Engels, 23
　and materialist dialectics,* 18
　as a science, 1–6, 7–8, 13, 14, 16, 17, 19, 20–21, 22, 27, 47, 66, 128, 135

Index

and the state,* 77
and women's rights, 120–121
See also Communism;* Ideology;*
Marxism; Materialist dialectics;*
Science; Socialism;* State*
History and Class Consciousness (G.
Lukacs), 61, 67. See also
Alienation*
*History of the Communist Party of
the Soviet Union—Short Course*
(J. Stalin, et. al.), 2, 3
Hitler, Adolf, 78
Holding company, 94
Homo sapiens, 10
Honduras, 99
How Europe Underdeveloped Africa
(W. Rodney), 110
Huntington, Samuel, 84

Ideology,* 1, 13, 32–33, 46, 87,
136, 139
bourgeois, 30
and the capitalist state, 71, 77–82,
86
and hegemony,* 80, 101, 135
and social production, 30–31, 34,
138
See also Alienation;* Capitalists,
ideology* of; Hegemony;*
Practice;* Relations of
production;* Superstructure*
IMF. See International Monetary
Fund
Imperialism,* 91, 107, 108, 135,
136
in Africa, 109
versus the environment, 104–105,
106, 108
Lenin on, 68, 98
Luxemburg on, 68
and neocolonialism,* 100–103,
108
versus peace, 103–104, 108
and socialism,* 118, 122
in Vietnam, 130
and war, 98–100
See also Africa, scramble for;
Capitalism,* advanced;
Capitalism,* monopoly;
Concentration; Finance
capital;* Labor,* aristocracy of;
Lenin; Neocolonialism*
*Imperialism: From the Colonial
Age to the Present*
(H. Magdoff), 108
*Imperialism: The Highest Stage of
Capitalism* (V.I. Lenin), 68, 98,
108
Inca Empire, 39
India, 39, 77, 96, 102, 122
Industrial reserve army, 63, 65
Infrastructure,* 117, 136, 139. See
also Superstructure*
Instruments of production, 34, 56,
57, 137
International capitalist system, 127
Internationalization of Capital, The
(B. Berberoghlu), 109
International Monetary Fund
(IMF), 100, 102, 103, 106,
108, 109, 110
International Telephone and
Telegraph (ITT), 95
International Workers of the World
(IWW), 129, 130
International Workingmen's
Association, 24
Introduction to Neo-Colonialism (J.
Woddis), 108
Inventing the People (E. Morgan),
85–86
Iroquois, 35
Islam, 89(n7)
Italy, 4, 77, 88
ITT. See International Telephone
and Telegraph

IWW. *See* International Workers of the World

Jalee, Pierre, 108
Japan, 75, 78, 84, 92, 102, 109, 123, 130
Joint Economic Committee of the U.S. Congress, 44–45
Jones, "Mother," 130
Junius Pamphlet (R. Luxemburg), 68, 87–88

Karl Marx: The Story of His Life (F. Mehring), 24
Kennedy, Joseph, 76, 99
Keynes, John Maynard, 103
Kore, Martin, 102
Korea, 104
Kotane, Moses, 109
Krupskaya, Nadezhda, 49

Labor,* 10, 29, 30, 36, 42, 46, 52, 54, 56, 57, 61, 64, 65, 94, 101, 116, 117, 126, 128, 134, 136, 138, 139, 140
  abstract, 4, 53, 54, 65, 135
  alienated, 60
  aristocracy of, 101, 107–108
  concrete, 4, 52, 53
  division of, 36, 37, 42, 49, 71–72, 81, 92, 107, 117, 119, 122, 126
  and labor-time, 97
  manual, 37, 119, 126
  movements, 5
  and necessary labor time,* 54, 59, 65, 66, 69, 137
  productivity of, 36, 39–40, 62, 91, 93, 107, 113, 115, 126, 134, 137
  reform, 75, 76, 83
  simple, 53
  skilled, 53
  slave, 36, 38, 39

violence, 76
See also Labor-power;* Labor theory of value;* Law of value;* Practice;* Socially necessary labor;* Surplus labor time;* Wage labor*
Labor-power,* 4, 56, 58, 59, 60, 61, 62, 64, 65, 66, 92, 97, 101, 134, 136, 137, 138, 139, 140. *See also* Capitalism;* Commodity;* Exploitation;* Labor;* Wage labor*
Labor theory of value,* 136
Lamarck, Jean Baptiste, 21
Latin America, 47, 97, 99, 100, 101, 102, 131
Law, 81
Lawner, Lynne, 89
Law of value,* 54, 65, 136
Lawrence, Massachusetts, 130
Lenin, Vladimir Ilyich
  on the aristocracy of labor, 101
  biographical note on, 48–49
  and the Bolshevik Revolution,* 133
  against bureaucracy,* 119, 124
  on class,* 42
  on communism,* 116–117, 119–120, 125, 126
  on the dictatorship of the proletariat,* 123
  on family relations, 121
  on imperialism,* 47–48, 94, 96, 98, 99, 108, 136
  and *Imperialism: The Highest Stage of Capitalism*, 68, 98
  and Luxemburg, 67–69
  on Marx, 21
  on Marxism, 2–3, 13, 17, 21, 30, 47, 113
  and *Materialism and Empirio-Criticism*, 11, 23
  and philosophy, 19, 23
  on politics, 77

Index

"On the Question of Dialectics," 41
  Rodney on, 91
  on socialism,* 115
  on Soviets,* 124
  and *The State and Revolution*, 74, 87, 115, 123, 134
  and *The Teachings of Karl Marx*, 48, 121
  See also Bolshevik Revolution;* Dictatorship of the proletariat;* Imperialism;* Krupskaya, N.
Leninism or Marxism? (R. Luxemburg), 68
Lent and Lost (Cheryl Payer), 109
Letters from Prison (A. Gramsci), 89
Liberty, 75
Liebnecht, Karl, 69
London, 23, 24
Los Angeles, 105
Ludwig Feuerbach and the Outcome of Classical German Philosophy (F. Engels), 22
Lukacs, Georg, 61, 67
Lumumba, Patrice, 109
Luxemburg, Rosa,
  biographical note on, 67–69
  against bureaucracy,* 119
  on democracy, 123, 125
  on the dictatorship of the proletariat,* 123
  and Lenin, 49, 67–69
  on Marx, 1
  and militarism, 103
  and political strategy, 77
  and *The Russian Revolution*, 87–88
  and socialism,* 108, 115
  and women's rights, 121
  See also Lenin

MacArthur, Gen. Douglas, 104
McCarthy era, 122
Machel, Samora, 110
Magdoff, Harry, 108
Maghoub, Ahmed, 110
Marine Corps (U.S.), 98–99
Market, 16, 51, 63, 91, 93, 113
  capitalist, 47, 51, 91, 93
  and communism,* 126–127, 128–129
  consumer, 76
  global, 47, 83, 97–98. *See also* Capitalism,* International
  and monopolies, 94–95. *See also* Capitalism,* monopoly
  and price,* 55
  relations,* 136, 137
  retail, 27
  and socialism,* 117–118
  stock, 43–44
  and supply and demand, 54, 63
  See also Capital;* Capitalism;* Commodity;* Exchange-value;* Price;* Relations of production;* Use-value*
Marx, Karl
  and analysis, 17, 51, 80
  on the "Asiatic mode of production," 39. *See also* Mode of production,* "Asiatic"
  biographical note on, 23–24
  and *Capital*, 29, 55–56, 64, 67, 94, 105, 136
  and *Civil War in France*, 88
  on communism,* 125
  and *Communist Manifesto*, 9, 47–48
  and *Critique of the Gotha Program*, 10, 125–126, 129
  and *Critique of Political Economy*, 32, 39
  and Darwin, 18, 19–20, 21
  on the *dictatorship of the proletariat*, 123–124, 134, 138
  and the "economic base," 32–33
  and *The Eighteenth Brumaire of Louis Bonaparte*, 88

Engels on, 130
and "the ensemble of social relations," 27
and *German Ideology*, 48
and *Grundrisse*, 48
and historical materialism,* 135, 137
and labor-power,* 59
Lenin on, 2, 21, 30, 48, 113, 121
Luxemburg on, 1, 67, 68
on "Marxists," 3
and materialism,* 7, 8, 15, 33
Mehring on, 3, 24, 47
on nature, 9–11, 105
and needs, 35, 59
on party organization, 129
and philosophy, 15, 19, 23
and his predecessors, 21, 22
and prediction, 19, 39, 40
and price,* 138
relations of production,* 34, 35
and social transformation, 17–19
on socialism,* 107
on the state,* 75, 77
and surplus value,* 58, 60
and *Theses on Feuerbach*, 23, 35
on *Wage Labor and Capital*, 67
and wants, 28–29
See also Engels, F.; *Capital*; *Civil War in France*; *Class Struggles in France*; Communist League; *Communist Manifesto*; *Critique of Political Economy*; *Critique of the Gotha Program*; *Economic and Philosophic Manuscripts of 1844*; *Eighteenth Brumaire of Louis Bonaparte*; First International; *Grundrisse*; Historical materialism;* Marxism; Marxists; Mehring, F.; *Teachings of Karl Marx* (V.I. Lenin); *Theories of Surplus Value*; *Theses on Feuerbach*; *Value, Price and Profit*; *Wage Labor and Capital*; Weydemeyer, letter to (K. Marx)

Marxism, 1, 4, 7, 22
in Africa, 109–110
and alienation,* 60–61
on class conflict, 75
on class divisions, 45
on class rule, 82, 83, 85. *See also* Class,* rule; Class,* ruling; State,* and class rule
and communism,* 113, 115, 120, 125–127, 128–129
debates within, 3
and dialectics, 17–19, 22, 41–42
Engels on, 22
and the Enlightenment, 9–10
and environmentalism, 5, 121–123
and family relations, 121
founders of, 39
as a guide to action, 4–5, 13, 16
and ideology,* 79, 81
on imperialism,* 109
and individual rights, 125
the influence of, 99
and knowledge, 13, 14–15
on labor-power,* 53, 56
and Lenin, 23, 48, 49, 68
and Leninists, 3
Lukacs on, 67
Luxemburg on, 49, 68
and materialism,* 8–17, 22
misrepresentations of, 1–2
and nature, 9–11, 105–106
and Neurath, 22
on the organic composition of capital, 62–63
"orthodox," 2, 3, 4, 21, 32
and positivism, 19–20
revisionist, 2
as a science, 5, 7, 19–20, 66

Index

and socialism,* 113, 114, 115–116, 118, 119
and society,* 27, 28, 31, 34, 46
and state power, 107
on stock ownership, 44
the study of, 5–6, 8
and value, 52, 54, 55
and women's rights, 120–121
See also Historical Materialism;* Marx;* Science
Massachusetts, 130
Materialism,* 8–17, 19, 21, 22, 31
and dialectics (materialist dialectics*), 18, 19, 137
See also Historical Materialism*
Materialism and Empirio-Criticism (V.I. Lenin), 11, 23
Materialist dialectics,* 18–19, 137
Mayer, Gustav, 24
Means of consumption,* 116, 117, 134. *See also* Commodity;* Means of production;* Means of subsistence
Means of production,* 34, 46, 65, 121, 137, 138
  capitalist, 55–56, 58, 62
  and class,* 42, 43, 72, 134
  and constant capital,* 62, 92, 133
  and socialism,* 115, 116, 117, 118, 126, 127
  and wage labor,* 140
  See also Capitalism;* Instruments of production;* Means of consumption;* Mode of production;* Productive forces;* Relations of production*
Means of subsistence, 28, 37, 59, 128. *See also* Means of consumption*
Mehring, Franz, 3, 24, 47, 67
Mercury (the planet), 10
Mexico, 99

City, 105
Middle Ages, 34, 55
Middle East, 38, 73, 104
  oil, 79
Military-industrial complex, 103–104
Minh, Ho Chi, 129, 130
Mode of production,* 37, 40, 46, 125, 137
  "Asiatic" (or tributary), 39, 137
  capitalist, 39, 51, 55, 56, 134
  characteristics of, 65–66
  and class,* 42, 134
  communist,* 113–114, 128, 134
  dominant, 42–43
  and economic structures,* 135
  feudal, 38
  and ideology,* 81
  and relations of production,* 117
  socialist,* 118
  and the state,* 74, 87
  See also Capitalism;* Communism;* Feudalism;* Mode of production,* "Asiatic"; Productive forces;* Relations of production*
Modern Prince (A. Gramsci), 89
Mondlane, Eduardo, 110
Money, 45, 51, 65, 103, 136
  and capital,* 60, 61, 94, 95, 96
  as a commodity,* 55, 69(n3)
  and communism,* 127
  and credit, 95–96
  in feudalism, 34, 38, 73
  and price,* 55, 138
  and stocks, 43, 44
  See also Capital;* Commodity;* Market, relations;* Price;* Exchange-value;* Wages*
Monopoly capitalism. *See* Capitalism,* monopoly;* Finance capital;* Imperialism*
Morgan, Edmund, 85–86

Moumie, Dr. Felix, 109
Mozambique, 110
Mussolini, 88

National City Bank, 99
Nature, 9–11, 21, 33, 81
Necessary labor time.* *See* Labor,* and necessary labor time
Neocolonialism,* 100, 107, 108, 136, 137
Neto, Agostinho, 110
Neurath, Otto, 14, 20, 22, 31
Newton, Isaac, 19
New York City, 129
Nicaragua, 99, 104
Nkrumah, Kwame, 100
"North," the, 102, 122
North America, 35, 76, 96, 102
Numeiri, 110
Nzula, Albert, 109

"On the Question of Dialectics" (V.I. Lenin), 23, 41
Organizational Questions of the Russian Social Democracy (R. Luxemburg), 68
Oriente province (Cuba), 130
Origin of Species (Charles Darwin), 21
Origin of the Family, Private Property, and the State (F. Engels), 87, 120
"Orthodox Marxists." *See* Marxists, "orthodox"
Ottoman Empire, 39
Ouande, Ernest, 109
Owen, Robert, 114–115

Palestine, 104
Palmer raids, 86
Paris, 24, 138
Paris Commune,* 47, 69, 88, 123, 124, 138

Payer, Cheryl, 109
People's History of the United States (H. Zinn), 84
People's Union of Cameroon (PUC), 109
Petty, William, 29
Philippines, 102
Pillage of the Third World (P. Jalee), 108
Pinochet, 78
Political Economy of Growth (P. Baran), 108
Popper, Karl, 20
Power. *See* State,* power
Practice (social practice),* 12–13, 28–33, 34–40, 46, 72–74, 75, 138, 139
  economic, 30, 31, 32, 33, 34, 39–40, 46, 66, 71, 81, 83, 138, 139
  and ideology,* 30, 31, 32, 33, 34, 71, 79, 81–82, 87, 136, 138, 139
  political, 31, 32, 33, 34, 41, 71, 72, 83, 86, 127, 138, 139
  See also Economic structure;* Ideology;* Infrastructure;* Productive forces;* Relations of production;* Superstructure*
Pre-Capitalist Economic Formations (K. Marx), 48
Price,* 27, 54–55, 57, 62, 63, 65, 91, 93, 101, 138
  and costs of production, 118
  of labor-power,* 56, 65, 66, 138
  and monopolies, 94
  and value, 138
  See also Capitalism,* and commodity production; Capitalists, and rate of profit; Commodity;* Exchange-value;* Supply and demand; Surplus value;* Wages

Index

Productive forces,* 4, 33, 46, 138
  and capitalism,* 38, 73
  and commodity production, 54
  and communalism, 72
  and communism,* 126
  and infrastructure,* 136
  and mode of production,* 46, 117, 137
  and relations of production,* 35, 138
  and socialism,* 115
  See also Instruments of Production; Means of Production;* Mode of Production;* Relations of Production;*
Profit
  and effective demand, 63
  motive, 57, 58, 73, 93, 126
  rate of, 16, 62, 64
  and socialism,* 117, 119
  and the stock market, 43–44
  and superprofits, 97, 100, 101
  and surplus value,* 58, 65, 66, 137, 139–140
  See also Capital;* Capitalism;* Effective Demand; Exchange-Value;* Exploitation;* Labor Power;* Market Relations;* Means of Consumption; Price;* Superprofits; Supply and Demand; Surplus value*
Proletariat. *See* Class,* working
Provisional government (of Russia), 133

Raw materials
  as capital,* 61–62, 64
  and capitalist production, 56, 57, 58, 63, 91, 92, 101
  and labor,* 29
  and means of production,* 34, 58, 137
  and monopolies, 94–95, 97
  and nature, 9–10
  See also Capital;* Commodity;* Instruments of production; Labor;* Means of production;* Nature; Practice;* Productive forces*
Reagan, Ronald, 104
Relations of (economic) production,* 4, 33–34, 35, 41, 46, 138
  capitalist, 78, 117, 126
  feudal, 73
  and ideology,* 79, 81
  Marx on, 123
  and mode of production,* 35, 46, 117, 135, 137
  and productive forces,* 35, 136
  See also Economic structure;* Exploitation;* Infrastructure;* Market relations;* Means of production;* Mode of production;* Productive forces;* Social relations; Structure (social)
Reminiscences of Lenin (N. Krupskaya), 49
Republican Party, 84
Ricardo, David, 21
Rodney, Walter, 39, 71, 91, 109, 110
Roman Empire, 38, 39
Rome, 34, 38, 40
Ruling class. *See* Class,* rule; Class,* ruling; State,* and class rule
Russia, 69, 87, 124, 133, 139
Russian Orthodox Church, 2

Saint Simone, Claude Henri de, 114
Sardinia, 88
Science, 1, 2, 4, 5, 7, 8, 10, 14, 16, 134
  and Darwin, 19–21

and Descartes, 22
and Galileo, 4
historical materialism and, 20–21, 22, 27, 30, 66, 67, 128, 135
Marx on, 48
Neurath on, 14, 22
positivists on, 19–20
social, 17–18, 33, 41, 47, 83, 85
as a social practice,* 31–32, 73, 74, 138
See also Historical materialism;* Materialism;* Materialist dialectics*
"Scientific communism," 2
Second International, 24
Siberia, 59
Smith Act, 130
Social Democratic Workers' Party, 129
Social formation,* 28, 139
Socialism,* 68, 79, 113, 115–119, 122, 128, 138
compared to communism,* 113–114
Lenin on, 113
Luxemburg on, 108
Marx on, 107, 129
utopian, 114–115, 120
and women, 121
as workers' power, 107, 114, 115, 119, 123, 126, 129, 130, 134, 138
See also Dictatorship of the Proletariat;* Utopian socialists
Socialism, Utopian and Scientific (F. Engels), 129
Socialist Party (of Italy), 88
Socially necessary labor.* *See* Labor,* and necessary labor time*
Social practice. *See* Practice*
Social relations, 13, 33, 34, 35, 42, 71–74, 78, 79, 81, 85, 87, 118, 123, 126, 127, 136

Marx on, 27
"South," 102, 105, 106, 109, 122
South Africa, 78, 109, 110
South African Communist Party, 109, 110
Southeast Asia. *See* Asia, Southeast; Philippines; Vietnam
Soviet* (workers' council), 124, 139
Soviet Union (USSR), 2, 103, 104, 125, 139
Constitution of, 131(n12)
and the dictatorship of the proletariat,* 123–124
and pollution, 106
and socialism,* 79, 105–106, 115
and women's rights, 120
"Speech at the Graveside of Karl Marx" (F. Engels), 22
Spinoza, Benedict, 12
Sri Lanka, 59
Stalin, Joseph
and communism,* 125
and the dictatorship of the proletariat,* 123–124
History of the Communist Part of the Soviet Union— Short Course, 2
and Krupskaya, 49
and Soviets,* 139
Standard Oil, 99
State, the*
and big business, 85, 107
and capitalism,* 47, 71, 73–77, 78, 79, 82, 85, 87, 89, 96, 101, 103
and class rule, 71–77, 83–84, 86–87, 127–128
and communism,* 113–114
and democratic centralism, 49
Engels on, 139
Hegel on, 137
and ideology,* 80, 82

Index 157

institutions of, 73, 74, 75, 82, 84, 85, 86, 87, 98, 109
and loans, 108
Marx on, 71
and militarism, 99, 103–104
and mode of production,* 74
power, 13, 49, 72, 74, 78, 87, 124, 128, 135
and self-determination, 68
and socialism,* 114, 115, 117–118, 125, 127
subsidies, 55, 101
and taxes, 61
See also Capitalists, as rulers; State capitalism*
State and Civil Society (A. Gramsci), 87, 88–89
State and Revolution (V.I. Lenin), 74, 87, 115, 123, 134
State capitalism,* 115, 139. *See also* Capitalism,* and planning; State*
State power. *See* State,* power
Structure (social), 19, 28, 32, 40, 46, 73, 140
  class, 46
  economic,* 30, 135
  power, 86
  of practices,* 31
  See also Historical materialism;* Infrastructure;* Mode of production;* Practice;* Superstructure;* Unity of opposites*
Sudan, 110
Suez Canal, 104
Summers, Lawrence, 105
Suni Muslims, 2
Superprofits, 97, 101, 108
Superstructure,* 32, 33, 46, 79, 136, 139
Supply and demand, 54, 63
Surplus labor time,* 137, 139

Surplus value,* 58–60, 61, 62, 64, 65, 66, 74, 78, 83, 93, 95, 104, 115, 133, 134, 135, 137, 139–140. *See also* Capitalism;* Exploitation;* Market, relations;* Profit; Surplus labor time*

Tampico, 99
Teachings of Karl Marx, The (V.I. Lenin), 48, 121
Technological determinism, 1, 2, 39, 93
Theories of Surplus Value (K. Marx), 67
Theses on Feuerbach (K. Marx), xi, 6, 23, 35
Tributary mode of production. *See* Mode of production,* "Asiatic"
Trilateral Commission, 84
Trotsky, Leon, 49
Trusts, 45, 75, 94, 96
Truth, 12, 81

United Nations (U.N.), 102
United States
  class divisions in, 44–45
  and class rule, 82–86, 96
  democracy in, 80
  as a "Great Power," 98–99
  and militarism, 103–104
  monopoly capitalism in, 40, 109, 115. *See also* Capitalism,* monopoly
  and pollution, 105
  slavery in, 42–43
  unions in, 130
  utopian communities in, 115
  See also Imperialism;* State,* and capitalism*
Unity of opposites,* 23, 41–42, 46, 140
Urban Land Institute, 84

Use-value,* 28–29, 46, 51, 52, 53, 54, 56, 136. *See also* Commodity;* Exchange-value*
Utopian socialists, 114–115, 120

Value. *See* Exchange-value*
Value, Price, and Profit (K. Marx), 67
Vanguard party, 49
Venus (the planet), 10
Vietnam, 104, 130

Wage labor,* 56, 66, 87, 114, 115, 134, 135, 139, 140. *See also* Capitalism;* Class,* working;* Labor;* Labor-power;* Relations of production;* Wages
Wage Labor and Capital (K. Marx), 67
Wages, 41, 42, 43, 45, 56–62, 64–65, 66, 92, 97, 130, 136, 137, 138, 140
  minimum, 75, 76
  piece, 56
  time, 56

and the World Bank, 105
See also Capitalism;* Labor-power;* Wage labor*
Wall Street, 99
Weydemeyer, letter to (K. Marx), 134
WHO. *See* World Health Organization
Woddis, Jack, 108
Wolfe, Bertram D., 68
Women's rights, 120–121
Working class. *See* Class, working
World Bank, 100, 102, 103, 105, 106, 108, 109
World Health Organization (WHO), 102
World War
  I, 69, 98, 108, 124
  II, 84, 99, 103, 130

Yerevan, 106

Zambia, 95
Zanzibar, 110
Zetkin, Clara, 67
Zinn, Howard, 84